Wrangling Women

WRANGLING

WOMEN

*Humor and Gender in
the American West*

Kristin M. McAndrews

 UNIVERSITY OF NEVADA PRESS

RENO & LAS VEGAS

University of Nevada Press
Reno, Nevada 895576 USA
Copyright © 2006 by University of Nevada Press
All rights reserved
Manufactured in the United States of America
Designed by Kathleen Szawiola

Library of Congress Cataloging-in-Publication Data

McAndrews, Kristin M., 1951–
Wrangling women : humor and gender in
the American west / Kristin M. McAndrews.— 1st ed.
p. cm.
Includes bibliographical references and index.
ISBN-13: 978-0-87417-683-4 (hardcover : alk. paper)
ISBN-10: 0-87417-683-2 (hardcover : alk. paper)
1. Horsemen and horsewomen—Washington (State)—Winthrop.
2. Sexism—Washington (State)—Winthrop.
3. Stereotype (Psychology)—Washington (State)—Winthrop.
4. Division of labor—Washington (State)—Winthrop. I. Title.
SF284.42.U6M33 2006
305.43'636100978—dc22   2006004715

The paper used in this book meets the requirements of
American National Standard for Information Sciences—
Permanence of Paper for Printed Library Materials,
ANSI Z.48–1984.
Binding materials were selected for strength and durability.

FIRST PRINTING

15 14 13 12 11 10 09 08 07 06
5 4 3 2 1

To Tony and Adam

There are things we do not tell
when we tell about weather
and being fine.
Our other voices take sanctuary
while police with their shepherds
stand guard
at the borders of breath
lest our stories escape
this holy building
of ourselves.

LINDA HOGAN
"The Other Voices"

Contents

Illustrations

Preface

Wrangling Women describes the ways in which some women who work with horses in the Methow Valley of eastern Washington State use humor in their storytelling and what this humor reveals about issues of gender in the American West. My discussion centers on a community of women who live in or near Winthrop, Washington, a western theme town. It concerns women working in a traditional community that, through tourism, perpetuates images of the American West—especially the cowboy. While women have long participated in the same activities as cowboys, they are often restricted or subordinated as active economic participants in the western landscape. When telling their stories, the women in this community employ traditional male narrative techniques but stretch or undermine these strategies by introducing nontraditional images and themes. And yet, while they do disrupt regional gender and narrative expectations, the stories often return to a community status quo. Though it is tempting to believe that by invading a male-dominated space, women's stories might lay bare social tensions and make open discussion and critique possible, in fact most of the tales conclude with an unspoken agreement to leave their subversive implications alone.

This project developed in a roundabout fashion. In the summer of 1991 my husband, Tony, and I were vacationing at Sun Mountain Lodge in Winthrop, Washington, which was the only major destination resort in the area at the time. On our last day there, we went on a horseback ride. As we hiked down a steep hill from the lodge, a young woman waved us over to the corral. She identified herself as Teresa and introduced the wrangler, whom I will call Cowboy Bob. Though Teresa was doing the talking while Bob saddled our horses, I just assumed he was in charge. After all his costume, weathered face, cowboy boots, and, most of all, his silence announced he was the cowboy and thus the authority. I soon realized, however, that I had misjudged the work dynamics. Teresa was the boss. When she didn't like the way Cowboy Bob was saddling my husband's horse, Widow Maker, Teresa began to tease Bob mercilessly. Eventually, she nudged him away from the horse and took over adjusting the cinch. Bob grumbled a bit, but after a minute or two he was laughing along with Teresa.

Bob was our guide for a one-hour trail ride through the many forested acres surrounding the lodge. Things suddenly became exciting when Cowboy Bob jumped off his horse and punched my horse, Fonzie, in the nose as punishment for nibbling some grass alongside the road. I held on to the saddle horn as the horse bucked furiously. In the meantime my husband (behind me) was pulling back on the reins of his horse, trying to get away from Fonzie's potentially lethal hooves. Unaware that his horse was angled to slip off the steep trail, Tony kept pulling back hard on the reins, and Widow Maker backpedaled in the dust. Finally noticing the probable horse wreck, Cowboy Bob shouted, "Let go of the reins." Tony dropped them, and his horse immediately stopped slipping. I didn't let go of the saddle horn for the rest of the ride.

Back at the corral, my husband and I watched Teresa and Bob treat a leg injury on another horse. A trained veterinarian's assistant, Teresa wanted to administer antibiotics, while Bob wanted to pack the wound with some salve he had brought. By laughing and teasing Bob for his stubbornness, Teresa eventually got him to do it her way. After Bob walked off grinning with the injured horse, I asked Teresa what her official title was at the lodge. She told me she was head wrangler of the horse concession. I was surprised, because I had thought "wrangler" was strictly a male designation. But Teresa said many women in the Methow Valley wrangled for a living, and I was intrigued to hear that women were working in such a physically demanding job.

In the summer of 1992 I began searching for cowgirls or horsewomen in Winthrop, Washington, which is a legally mandated western theme town. At first I looked for women who made their livings primarily by working with horses, and by 1994, through word of mouth from one woman to another,

I knew of many working horsewomen in the Methow Valley. This surprised and delighted me. What I had believed to be a staunchly male working domain contained many more women than I expected—women working physically as hard as any cowboy, packer, or wrangler I met while also taking care of their families. The horsewomen I interviewed had pragmatic and optimistic approaches to life. Through creativity and concentrated effort, these women sustained themselves economically, a small, not particularly affluent community in the Methow Valley, while still pursuing their passion for riding horses. Between 1996 and 2000 I expanded my interviews to include women who held other jobs but had significant connections to horses through their professions, recreational competitions, ranching, or packing into the wilderness. In 2000 I took photographer Karen Cowdrey to visit several of the women I had interviewed. Karen took photos of significant moments in their work with horses and their daily activities. Eleven years after my starting this project, other residents of the Methow Valley still tell me of women I could interview— "real" cowgirls. Several women I contacted chose not to be interviewed. Not all the members of this traditional community are particularly open to inviting strangers (especially of the academic variety) into their homes.

Transcription proved to be a major challenge. My first transcriber completed two tapes but quit before finishing the third. My second transcriber quit as well, with the excuse that what I wanted in terms of transcription was too difficult. At this point I personally confronted the truth of Richard Bauman's remark that "beyond the matter of discourse and performance structures, one faces additional problems, partly analytical, partly ethical, in rendering spoken language in written form" (1986, ix). Having initially discovered few narratives of cowgirls or horsewomen, I wanted to show my respect for all of their words by reproducing the entire oral text. I thought that all the narrative blips and blurbs; the *um*'s, *uh*'s, and *ah*'s and the repetitions; and even the informants' western accents should somehow appear in the written versions. A third transcriptionist quit, and then a fourth. I finally decided to do the job myself—an enjoyable exercise.

But when I looked at the drafts prepared this way, I decided that the verbal stutters and narrative skips actually impeded access to the social and generic concerns I was most interested in foregrounding. Thus, the stories are presented

as told, but with the halts or stumbles removed and without an attempt to reproduce pronunciation accurately, though in some of them I have indicated the
phonetic form of the women's western accents. I have also added notes to explain
unfamiliar images or geographical locations. As much as possible, given the purposes of the study, the transcriptions record the words in the order in which they
were spoken by the cowgirls/horsewomen I interviewed. I have titled most of the
stories as a matter of convenience for the ensuing discussion.

I feel very fortunate to have enjoyed time with many talented and hardworking women in the Methow Valley. I am grateful to my writing group, Kaethe
Kauffman, Susan Scott, and Jennifer Crites, who made thoughtful suggestions
on the manuscript. My thanks to Cristina Bacchilega, Craig Howes, Nancy
Youngren, and Karen Cowdrey for their enthusiasm and support. My deepest
appreciation and love to Tony and Adam, to whom this book is dedicated.

Enjoy the ride.

Wrangling Women

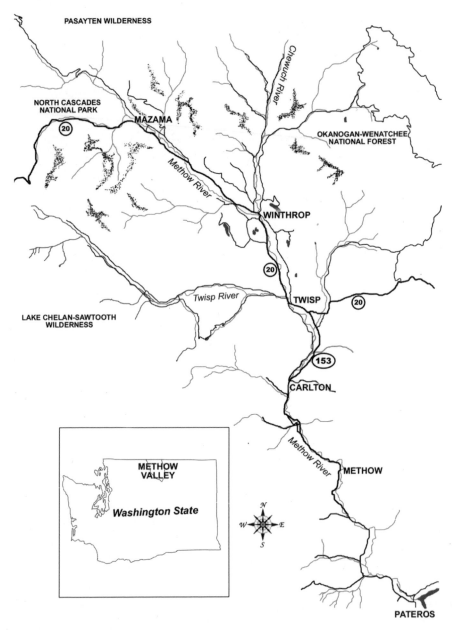

Map of Methow Valley. Courtesy of Dawn Woodruff,
Medicine Wheel Website Design, Inc.

INTRODUCTION

Cowgirls—Subversive Implications

Remember Dale Evans? You know, the cowgirl who was kind of Roy Rogers's sidekick, but not quite? Dale Evans was my first cowgirl memory, and I loved her. High in the saddle, riding with confidence and grace, she was a powerful role model. Comfortable with danger—I considered riding a horse very dangerous—she could even lasso bad guys and cows. I always wished for more stories in which Dale was the main character. I wanted her to win a few gunfights, to wrestle a couple of villains to the ground. As a woman in western and 1950s American culture, though, it wasn't her traditional job to be the heroic figure. Though she accompanied Roy on some excellent adventures, more often than not she was back in town, taking care of the boys at the café—cooking and cleaning up while always looking terrific. On *The Roy Roger and Dale Evans Show*, Dale straddled two worlds: the cowboy world, which made her look capable, equal, an individual—a feminist, if you will—and the domestic world, where all good women lived—competent, silent, and usually apart from men. Though fictional, the cowgirl world of Dale Evans represented something inherently true about the historical roles of women in American culture. Independence is generally accepted as long as we're not too loud and as long as dinner is on time, the kids are clean, and the laundry is folded and stowed. Equality within limits—feminism without conflict.

Like Dale Evans, the women in this book strongly identify with the American West. But initially I struggled with how to distinguish the talented and hardworking women of the Methow Valley, to bring their lives into some sort of relationship with images of the American West. Were they cowgirls or cowboy-girls? Strictly speaking, none of the women I interviewed performed the work of a cowboy—which technically should be the rounding up and moving of cattle. "People who have worked with cattle for a long time are picky about how loosely the term cowboy or cowgirl gets used," Virginia Bennett, ranch manager and cowboy poet, told me: "There was a time where I wouldn't even call someone who worked in the rodeo or who rode broncs a cowboy. Or those mountain guide dudes, you don't call them a cowgirl or cowboy. It's got the word 'cow' in there, so it has got to do with cattle" (2000). But seventy-two-year-old Babe Montgomery, a local horse trainer, argued that the work of cowboys and cowgirls has changed, with tourists symbolically replacing cattle (1994). While some of the women I interviewed had experience moving cattle, many worked in tourist-related jobs. These women handle horses, and sometimes livestock, but they also work as horse trainers, veterinarians, dude-ranch owners and managers, cooks, packers, musicians, artisans, teachers, hotel employees, and office workers. And frequently, they also perform the majority of domestic and child-rearing tasks within their homes.

So are these women cowgirls? "Cowgirl" seems a diminutive of cowboy, although historically they did the same kind of work. Generally though, the women I interviewed resisted being identified strictly as cowgirls. Then should I have referred to them as "women wranglers"? When I asked, they generally agreed that the term was derogatory and did not reflect their styles of working with horses—although many of the women still refer to themselves as wranglers anyway. But when I suggested "horsewoman" as a possible identification, there was a general consensus. Though when I asked Shiril Cairns, she was quiet for a minute and then said, "Well, it would depend on the horse" (1992).

Since this book discusses the language of women in relation to dominant notions of the American West, I must move back and forth between using "cowgirl" and "horsewoman." Throughout however, I keep in mind Dale Evans's claim that "cowgirl is an attitude, really. A pioneer spirit, a special American brand of courage . . . a cowgirl might be a rancher, or a barrel racer, or a bull rider or an actress. But she's just as likely to be a checker at the local Winn-Dixie, a full-time mother, a banker, an attorney, an astronaut" (Gilchrist 1993, iii). In the Methow Valley women who work with horses and tourists necessarily have an attitude—courage, ingenuity, a good sense of humor, and a facility with language.

When I began to research the history and folklore of the cowgirl, I came to the same conclusion as Dale Evans. "I never felt the cowgirl received enough attention," she says in *Cowgirls: Women of the Wild West*, "Outside of Calamity Jane and Annie Oakley, there were very few cowgirls people knew about" (Flood 2000, 9). But I did find useful texts. *The Cowgirls* by Joyce Gibson Roach provides historical accounts of women who lived on the frontier at the turn of the century, concluding with biographical information largely drawn from the archives at the Cowgirl Hall of Fame, which was then located in Hereford, Texas.[1] Roach's text focuses on women who rodeoed in the early to mid-twentieth century. Teresa Jordon's *Cowgirls: Women of the American West*, a collection of narratives from women working on ranches, wrangling for ranch owners, and rodeoing, is also insightful. In *Cowgirls of the Rodeo: Pioneer Professional Athletes*, Mary Lou LeCompte focuses on women in the rodeo from Wild West shows to the early 1990s.[2] Until the 2002 publication of Joan Burbick's *Rodeo Queens and the American Dream*, however, few folkloric or feminist works discussed storytelling in relationship to the cowgirl or horsewoman experience. When Burbick interviewed former rodeo queens from the Lewiston Roundup in Idaho, their "memories and lives" forced her to "rethink the history and culture of the American West" (2002, 2). On my recent check of the Library of Congress, there were 3,196 entries on the cowboy and 172 items on cowgirls.

While I became accustomed to the absence of cowgirl narratives, I had assumed that women's use of humor would be an essential part of humor studies. What a surprise to discover—women were not funny. As a doctoral candidate, I took a course on humor. My initial impression of the course materials was that while information on how and why men employ humor seemed abundant, by omission or explicitly, humor studies assumed women didn't have a sense of humor. When I dug further, I found few publications or articles on women's use of humor and only one on women and the tall tale.[3] At this point I began to suspect that the reason there was so little scholarship on women's humor was that male researchers didn't understand it, or perhaps they didn't recognize it. Robbie Davis Johnson's "Folklore and Women: A Social Interactional Analysis of the Folklore of a Texas Madam" provided support for my assumptions. Johnson notes that Hilda, a Texas madam, and her employees believed their language skills were the most important tools of their job for maintaining control over their male clientele (1973, 211–24), and that also explained how humor was one of the most effective ways of assuming this control. I recalled Teresa's laughing, teasing, and coercing of Cowboy Bob and began to wonder if women who work successfully in male-dominated fields generally use humor manipulatively.

The lack of scholarship on cowgirls and on women's use of humor ultimately inspired this project of collecting humorous and frightening horse-related stories from women living in or near Winthrop, Washington. My research began with phone calls to people I had met while on vacation in the valley, asking them for names of women who made their livings primarily by working with horses. I discovered that Teresa had left the Methow Valley, but I did get the names of six women who fit the profile. Three women responded to my letters—Pat Miller, Babe Montgomery, and Judy Mally-Burkhart. Though it turned out that Pat Miller didn't make her living with horses—her husband, Claude Miller, was an outfitter—she gave me the names of Marva Mountjoy and of Ann Henry, who cooked regularly for her husband's outfitting business. When I arrived in the Methow Valley in June of 1992, I personally contacted those potential interviewees who hadn't replied to my letters. In addition I called an old friend, Debbie Tolton, who raises Arabian horses, in Republic, Washington, some 150 miles northeast of Winthrop. She agreed to be interviewed and gave me the names of three women in the Republic area who also proved willing.

As a freelance writer in Honolulu for two and a half years, I had interviewed dozens of people for local magazines and newsletters. But since I had never done an oral history, I sought out scholarship on collecting stories.[4] Even at this early stage, however, I had reservations about the "scientific," objective approach that more often than not is advanced in folklore studies. Sustaining this objective point of view and the linked emotional distance as another woman described her experiences and feelings would be a profound challenge, especially when the project emerged in part out of my sincere admiration and identification with these women. Nevertheless, during the first series of interviews I kept the required distance from my informants, revealing little about myself. I simply assumed that I could collect the information I desired while remaining detached. The community itself led me to believe this was the polite approach as well.

Since eastern Washington State tends to be socially and politically conservative, in all my formal interviews I assured the women that I wasn't interested in anything "personal." Since the population is small, people are apt to be quite private, and I did not want to appear too intrusive. And finally, I was conducting these interviews during the summer, the busiest time of year for the women and their community. These women were already being especially generous with their time. I didn't want to push.

Conversations took place mostly in the women's homes but also next to a lake, in a saddle shop, at a corral, in a bookstore, and in a veterinarian's office. While most of the women I talked to had not been interviewed before, Judy Mally-Burkhart and Shiril Cairns had been featured in magazines or newspaper articles profiling their businesses, Early Winters Saddle Shop and Rocking Horse Ranch. Marva Mountjoy had been the focus of an extensive article in *Western Horsemen*. Kit McLean Cramer, who works at the horse concession at Sun Mountain Lodge, has been featured in the *New York Times*'s Sunday Travel Section, two *Sunset Magazine* articles, and a Japanese advertisement promoting the Northwest. Lauralee Northcott and Virginia Bennett, gifted writers, storytellers, and members of a girl band called Horse Crazy, had also given interviews, primarily promoting their music and writing. Lauralee collects narratives from visitors to specific wilderness sites in the surrounding area. Virginia is an accomplished cowboy poet and writer who has published two books of poetry, *Canyon of the Forgotten* and *Legacy of the Land: Cowboy Poetry*.[5] She has also been a regular performer at the Cowboy Poetry Gathering in Elko, Nevada. Meghan Sullivan (Shiril Cairns's daughter) and her ranch were featured in the *Ruralite*, a regional magazine.[6] Meghan's portrait, entitled "Wrangler at Rocking Horse Ranch," was also part of a spring 2003 art short at the Confluence Gallery in Twisp, Washington, ten miles east of Winthrop, featuring the impressionist oil painter, Mary Powell.

Each woman was enthusiastic and sometimes suspicious; their interviews ran from one to eight hours. My first interviews refined my collecting skills and my theoretical assumptions. I had begun with the idea that women working in male-dominated professions (especially cowboy culture) would use language subversively to manipulate men they worked with or for. Since humor is often described as a subversive and aggressive mode of discourse, I simply assumed that horsewomen would have dynamic senses of humor because of their work with horses and their cultural positions. Several of the horsewomen did prove to be outspoken, irreverent, and funny, yet at least during this first phase, while some informants were entertaining, they were hardly overwhelmingly humorous. Perhaps, however, the fault was mine. To understand their humor, I had to become more involved with their community. For this reason, the focus of the book is the Methow Valley. To understand the complex cultural dynamics of these women and the humor they employ in storytelling, I found it necessary to commit myself to this geographic location.

Having interviewed several women in the Methow Valley, in 1994 I began to search more extensively for historical accounts and images of working cowgirls. In the regional museum in Okanogan, Washington, I looked for stories by women about other women or about themselves. No historical cowgirls and, in fact, only a few women's stories appeared. I repeated the same process in the archives of Shafer Museum, in Winthrop, with the same results. Though women clearly played an integral part in the settlement and economic development of the town, few published narratives recorded their lives. What I did learn, however, was how tenacious and pervasive the justifications for this absence were. When I commented to the retired women who worked as tour guides at the Okanogan County Historical Museum on how few female narratives were in the archives, they would reply that this should have been expected, since what men do, or have done, is so much more important than women's work. When I occasionally suggested that women might make better decisions about their lives if they heard more stories about the life experiences of other women, some of the retirees seemed to feel the idea was dangerous, while others took my remarks as an invitation to share their own horrendous stories of abuse and neglect.

My research into issues of gender in American folklore, humor studies, and the American West therefore produced few women's tales. Even within collections of personal narratives, the women often seemed missing, thanks in part to the overpowering male ideological presence in the critical discourse available to assess them. Barbara Babcock explains this phenomenon: "For centuries 'woman' has been figured by male philosophers and social theorists as disorder, savagery, chaos and unreason—as the excluded 'other' by which structure constitutes itself" (1993, 60). In the American West women have also paradoxically been restricted by being pulled to the opposite pole as purveyors of order and culture. Carol Mitchell claims, "western patriarchal ideology has created cultural lenses that emphasize males, hierarchy, dualism, and linear/logical ways of knowing" (1993, 281). As for women, Claire Farrer argues:

> The image of women dominant in American folkloristics is one of creatures confined to home and hearth, conversant with charms and cures and possessing various quaint beliefs. . . . At times woman was seen as a danger, a witch; other times she was a frivolous child interested in games. She may have known and bequeathed a rich traditional heritage, but information is sketchy concerning the extent of her folklore repertoire. Her image was that of homebody; her behavior, even in areas outside the home, was consistent with her image. (1975, xvi)

When I began trying to place Babe Montgomery, Shiril Cairns, Jessie Dice, Meghan Sullivan, Lauralee Northcott, or Virginia Bennett's stories within folklore studies, I soon found myself agreeing with Carol Mitchell and Farrer. In the fields of both folklore and humor studies, women's narratives are programmatically diminished. As Dan Ben-Amos explains, the ways folklore distinguishes types of stories often reflect a gender politics of speech, resulting in generic taxonomies that "are reflections of the rules for what can be said in what situation, in what form, by whom and to whom (1969, 285). While this concept is changing, in many folkloric and oral-history studies speaking women are often assumed to be unreliable narrators or described as minimally expressive. And within the realm of male and female storytelling, Farrer notes that "we have 'tall tales,' a male genre of storytelling; the female corollary is exaggeration. Men have 'stories' or 'yarns': women have 'gossip' or 'clothes lining'" (1975, xvi).

The critical perception that women are minimally or trivially expressive is due in part to a denial that women have a distinct culture. Though any claim that women share pervasive gender values must be heavily qualified, women share certain biological connections that it would be foolish not to assume have some effect on our storytelling. Furthermore, our shared experience of biological facts, which have traditionally led to socially and culturally constructed codifying gender roles, also grant us something in common. Even when we are the primary wage earners while performing our roles as child bearers and homemakers, we are still allocated to a subordinate sphere of influence—the domestic. Or as Dawn Currie and Valerie Raoul put it, "gender divisions along sexual lines were portrayed as universally beneficial. . . . In the study of history, economics, politics or culture, the activities and experience of men were taken as the norm. Women and their experiences were either ignored or portrayed as deviations from the male standard" (1992, 1).

Of course the way to explore the presence of women is to talk to them—women collecting stories from women. And "the female subculture has often been a defense against, and a critique of, male dominance," as Susan Armitage observes; "the very act of focusing on women and asking them to 'speak for themselves' is a challenge to traditional male-centered history" (1987, 4). The problem lies in the preexisting disparities in power and value. In a culture that marks the dominant and the public as male and the subordinate or domestic as female, stories collected by women from women about women are marginalized or ignored.

I took the advice of folklorist Charles Briggs, who counsels a working interaction with informants. Instead of passively and objectively collecting stories, researchers must study the work and interests of the informants. If they carve statues, the field-worker learns to carve (1986). In my case, if women ride horses or pack into the wilderness and then do the laundry, then the field-worker does too. Only then can one know what questions to ask. Given the goals of my project, Briggs made a great deal of sense. After all, how could I hope to understand these active, engaged women without making a whole-hearted attempt to learn something about the conditions of their lives?

Since beginning this project, I have taken pack trips into the wilderness surrounding the Methow Valley and have spent two months off and on riding "cowgirl" with Kit McLean Cramer. I have also taken numerous trail rides throughout the valley. Janet Boyce and Terry DeWeert set up a cow-cutting demonstration so I could observe the riding techniques involved. Terry explained:

> You have a herd of cows, and four people kinda helping you keep your herd and the cow organized, that you're going to cut out. But the cutter [the rider] has to go into the herd without disturbing it and pull out one cow or, they [the riders] can push out the whole herd and hold one cow out. For a time period of at least two and a half minutes, they have to cut out two cows and keep it held out away from the herd, or else you lose points. The more points you lose the more points you lose in your class. But each movement the cow makes the horse is mimicking it. The horse is completely trained to the point that the rider drops the reins, then the horse is down and moving so quick back and forth on that cow that you're pushing yourself back in the saddle. If you use your hands at all to direct your horse, you get points off.
>
> It gets wild and crazy. It's the biggest adrenaline rush you've ever had. (1999)

After witnessing the cow-cutting event, I had no impulse to try cow cutting, as separating a cow from the herd looked like physically demanding and extremely dangerous work. Though by no stretch of the imagination an expert, I do feel I gained a better understanding of these women's professional routines and competitive activities. I also became increasingly aware of my own role as a specific kind of audience for a community-inflected performance. As I became more open to my informants, I grew more sensitive to the ways in which humor did in fact function subversively with the horsewomen's tales, and I learned more about the specifics of the women's gendered position in Winthrop. While my subjects did not gossip about other women in the valley, for example, people had opinions about how certain women handled animals—from cats to cattle. Virginia Bennett told me that some people thought she treated her horses like pets—very well-trained pets. Virginia could stand on the back of her stock-still horse with her boots on. Although on another

Terry DeWeert cow cutting on the Rendezvous, 2000.
Photograph courtesy of Karen Cowdrey

occasion, the same horse had bitten her breast when she was teaching him to kiss her on the lips (2000). Shiril Cairns also knew that people thought her horses were spoiled—not that she cared one bit:

> One of the vets down in Twisp described my horses as poodles because they are so mellow. I don't like a horse I can't catch. Up here people say 'You don't touch that horse until he's three! Yah break him rough. If ya gotta have a board meeting with him, ya get yourself a two by four!' Sure, if you want broken bones, do it that way! Yeah, then you can prove yourself and just how strong, etcetera, you are.
>
> It's all in the approach. I think women are different. I think women take less of the conqueror attitude and more of a cooperative attitude with horses. But I know there are also some women who work the opposite way. (1992)

Through my study, though I have learned a great deal about my interview subjects' lives and horses and their community, I paradoxically became more

Virginia Bennett trained by horse, 2000.
Photograph courtesy of Karen Cowdrey

aware of certain unbridgeable gaps between the women and myself. To begin with, though now familiar with their work routines, I am myself a cowgirl wanna-be, without any real expertise in the horsewomen's "horse-related" lives. As a working wife and mother, I do claim some identification with these women's domestic lives, and because I own property in the valley, I have a strong interest in political and recreational development issues.[7] I also take advantage of the hiking, fishing, camping, biking, and skiing opportunities enjoyed by residents and tourists alike.[8] As an American woman, I understand the pervasive stereotypes of cowboy culture that are held fast within our society. And further, I comprehend the difficulty of opening a controversial gap in what the community views as its basic folkloric identity.

Winthrop, like so many other small towns, is not particularly open to strangers. Permanent residents are still treated as outsiders twenty years after they arrive; tourists and absentee homeowners like me never really cross into the community's inner social circle. Property in the Methow Valley is also expensive, with rental housing difficult to find, making the house I built in the fall of 1992, empty most of the year, a possible source of resentment for Winthrop workers. When I add in my role as academic tourist, bent on ingesting elements of the community to nourish my own work, the distance from my informants becomes more evident—but with a compensating gift.[9] My own vexed but self-conscious interviewing position helped me become more aware of the various positions occupied by my interviewees as women, citizens of Winthrop, and cultural workers.

Another methodological difficulty in this kind of project is deciding upon the most suitable governing discipline for discussion. Do I ground my discussion in literature? Oral history? Folklore? Anthropology? Gender studies? Humor studies? American history? All at once? What I soon realized was that these disciplines share that common habit of rendering women invisible by not discussing them. Amy Shuman declares that folklore and cultural studies lean toward the essentializing of women. Since "male" is "the unmarked variety, standing for 'people,' culturally," and therefore is "the marked variety upon which value is conferred," women are marked for their invisibility (1993, 346–47). But my training in literary criticism did not necessarily seem any better suited to the task. Although transcription often appeared to make the horsewomen's stories recognizably literary, their disciplinary status became ambiguous because they emerged from the mouth rather than from the pen. And as Richard Bauman observes: "Scholars in literature departments operate within a frame of reference dominated by the canons of elite, written, Western literary traditions and texts, which tends to restrict consideration of oral literature to a search for sources and analogues of more cultivated literature" (1986, 1). Discussing the cowgirl's stories through a traditional textual point of view therefore always runs the risk of subordinating these women's experience to more literary concerns. While discussions of women's fiction and oral narratives are changing, the dominant academic tendency still moves toward treating female storytelling as gossip, which places a woman's oral aesthetic at a disadvantage within a literary landscape.

For instance, though some of the horsewomen's stories contain easily recognizable elements of the tall tale, the contemporary legend, and the joke, critical discussion of these subgenres, at least in practice, tends to omit or

marginalize female characters. I've also found that any notion of unprob-
lematically or empirically collecting social data gets complicated by the town
of Winthrop. Though the stories contain important cultural and social elements, they are also accounts of female work experience as refracted through
tourism. For example, Winthrop has laws requiring westernized storefronts.
While this makes the town an ideal site for examining contemporary frontier
tourism, it also becomes the implicit comic butt of community decision making, tourism in general, and the present tourist-inflected listener—me—not
the ideal control situation for social scientific analysis.

In response to the disciplinary obstacles, throughout this text I resist all
impulses to provide definitive categories or explanations for stories told to me
by the Methow Valley horsewomen. Their lives are too socially and economically complex for such arrogance. What I think I can offer, however, is another
point of view from which to consider women's storytelling and humor by following the example of D. Diane Davis:

> I-write for those thinkers who are more interested in slow reflection than in
> "gaining time," who are more interested in ethical re-valuation than in "eco-
> nomic calculation." I-write for those who, in spite of everything, will have appre-
> ciated breaking up, cracking up, busting up; those who will have appreciated
> (longed for?) a community, a pedagogy, and a politics that begins t/here, from a
> finite and disidentified fluidity that will have been "us," that will have been who
> "we" are. (2000, 4)

And feminism is a part of this writing process. One of the ethical challenges I have wrestled with has been to represent these women without burying them in the rhetoric of folkloristics, oral history, feminist theory, studies
of humor, and the history of the American West. Since such women's narratives are relatively rare, I want to make them available in ways that acknowledge the tellers' substantial contributions to their community and to culture
at large. And yet, even as I attempt to adopt a more open, feminist approach
to fieldwork and folklore, the existing disciplines still pull on me, making the
stories less autonomous—more subsumed in a larger ideological discourse.
This problem has often been noted. Rachelle Saltzman suggests that the
"contradictions inherent in combining folkloric and feminist perspectives,"

both in conducting fieldwork and analyzing data, exist "largely because folk-lore theory and research have tended to have privileged male informants and masculine forms of expressive culture—even when women and their lore are examined" (1993, 51). Debra Kodish points out that practical guides for doing folklore fieldwork are often silent about gender issues; she goes on to suggest that if we read "this absence as an ideological presence," we can then not only deconstruct male paradigms, but create models attentive to women's experience (1993, 15). Arguing that a feminist approach is a more balanced method for collecting and discussing oral texts, Miriam Camitta urges field-workers to recognize the subjective nature of what dominant culture perceives as "pure science." Observer and informant should emotionally connect; field-workers should be friends, not scientists (1990, 21–31).

But then there's Judith Stacey, whose initial support for a feminist model for ethnographic research faded when in practice she found the paradigm as restrictive and exploitive—and perhaps more so—as masculinist interviews. Although verbal intimacy or friendship and knowledge between researcher and informant should allow a truth to emerge, Stacey warns that "the greater the intimacy—the greater the apparent mutuality of the researcher/researched relationships—the greater the danger" (1991, 114). Exploitation and betrayal of confidence are always possible, and to be true to its own assumptions, research following principles of feminist ethnography must acknowledge the researcher's self-reflective contribution to the storyteller's performance. Even when one seeks a "neutral description" of a folk idea, political ideologies lurk within. Shuman states, "the category 'folk' is never neutral, we can identify the positions, politics and interests that are involved in negotiating and maintaining its boundaries" (1993, 359). Given these considerations, I resolved to collect and present the narratives in a way that above all does justice to this particular group of women, focusing on their articulated experiences while remaining aware of the coercive and directing potential not only in the patriarchal, scientific ideological frame of the academy, but in the feminist assumptions underlying my attempts to escape somewhat from that frame as well.

And then there is the town. An economic necessity in the Methow Valley, tourism has had a tremendous impact on the women I interviewed. Tour-

Horses at Sun Mountain corral, 2000. Photograph courtesy of Karen Cowdrey

ism in the American West has a surprisingly long history. According to Dee Brown, "Westerners were quick to realize the attractions of the 'wild and wooly' for adventure-hunting Easterners, and the opportunity for commercial exploitation of 'adventure' was particularly favorable in the border states" (1995, 354–55). Each year tourists from around the world visit western theme towns "to drink in its meaning, to be restored by its atmosphere" (Anne Butler 1994, 776). The American West has been commodified, as it embodies attractive national values and virtues. Visitors take photos of the picturesque and buy cowboy memorabilia—often manufactured in foreign countries. In western theme towns across the country today, cowboy culture carries on the tradition of catering to the tourist fantasy by apparently integrating the tourist into this culture, yet it preserves the community's integrity by actually keeping the tourist at an often invisible arm's length.

Women face a double challenge in catering to tourists since, from its earliest representations, western culture has denied women's participation in cowboy occupations and has trivialized their abilities with language. As Jane Tompkins explains, "The Western man's silence functions as a script for behavior; it expresses and authorizes a power relation that reaches into the farthest corners of domestic and social life. The impassivity of male silence suggests the inadequacy of female verbalization, establishes male superiority, and silences the one who would engage in conversation" (1993b, 52). Much of the responsibility for the stereotypic images of western women as submissive but chatty and western men as strong, willful, and silent can be placed on the shoulders of Owen Wister, father of the western novel and probably Winthrop's most famous historical tourist. His novel *The Virginian* (1902) inspired an entire genre of literature that granted women a facility with the language of emotion but firmly barred women from the wilderness, as a landscape too rough for their emotional natures. Men wanted to be alone there in the wilderness, for as Tompkins claims, "women, like language, remind men of their own interiority; women's talk evokes a whole network of familial and social relationships and their corollaries in the emotional circuitry" (1993b, 57). For western men's exclusive fraternity, the wilderness is somehow indistinguishable from virility and general health. It is this vision that Winthrop now seeks to invoke through its western facades and tourist industry, but as my interviews often confirmed, equally traditional dismissive attitudes toward women find their expression as well. While the horsewomen's demeanor and lifestyle suggest the possibility of equal incorporation into images of the American West, as women they are excluded from full membership.

In the following chapters I describe how a recognizable folkloric pattern of horsewomen's humor conducts elemental critiques of the local community, images of the American West, and issues of popular culture by taking a position heavily conditioned by gender. What necessarily emerge are new images of working women, formed in response to that pervading image of the American West as it has been traditionally framed through literary and historical discourse. As I describe what can be thought of as the horsewoman's aesthetic and expose the framework of such female narratives, I remain aware of Carol Mitchell's warning that "all scholarship is political, for it reflects an unconscious as well as a conscious ideology" (1993, 281). Nevertheless, while acknowledging the limitations of my cultural and ideological perspective, I will seek to present the horsewoman's narratives, her humor, and her culture in an ethical and yet nonjudgmental manner.

CHAPTER ONE

TOURISM, GENDER, AND IMAGES OF THE AMERICAN WEST

After a rush through a seemingly vast and beautiful wilderness via the North Cascades Highway (U.S. Route 20 East), tourists drop into the center of the Methow Valley and historic Winthrop, Washington. As venues for recreation and leisure and for exploring those cultural icons, the cowboy and his rugged lifestyle, both the highway and Winthrop lend themselves well to tourist culture. Though the highway was originally intended to forge commercial links in eastern Washington and to stimulate mining activities in the Methow Valley, almost immediately "tourism became a more lucrative prospect than prospector's gold," and with its sweeping, spectacular views and many lookout points, the road shows unmistakable signs of a planned tourist attraction (Portman 1993, 112). The designers succeeded. Sally Portman calls the highway "one of the most scenic arterials in the world," and Winthrop tourist pamphlets often tout it as the "Gateway to the American Alps."

Anticipating the completion of the North Cascades Highway in the early 1970s, the once nondescript mining, logging, and cattle town of Winthrop began embracing the image of the American West by transforming itself into a western theme town. Its "western-style face-lift" was already well underway "when the governor cut the ribbon" to open the road in September of 1972.

Soon "new businesses in town began to attract tourists, and the town's economy boomed" (Portman 1993, 113–14). Within a tourist economy, having a theme for your town is in a sense more important than exactly what the theme is. Otto and Kathryn Wagner, longtime residents and the prime movers for Winthrop's western theme, actually based their arguments on the successful renovation of Leavenworth, Washington, into a Bavarian village, and although the Wagners themselves, who seemed more interested in appearance and public spirit than economics, "never considered tourism an important reason for restoring Winthrop, the merchants and city government surely did" (Portman 1993, 171). Soon architects, planners, and organizers were studying towns and scanning through old photos of western-style buildings, and even of old Winthrop itself, for images that would "make the design as authentic as possible" (Portman 1993, 172). Today, Winthrop is a legally mandated western town. All businesses within the city limits must adhere to guidelines, which control everything from a structure's architectural style to the lettering and color of the paint on the display sign out front. One convenience-store owner told me that at first the council rejected his proposed western motif because of the words "mini-mart" on his sign. A change to "first-mart" was proposed, and in order to open his business, the owner complied. Later, the owner appealed the "first-mart" designation, and the original ruling was reversed.

The dependence on tourism, complicated by such pervasive, culturally loaded images as those of the American West, can have tremendous consequences for a small community. In *Devil's Bargains: Tourism in the Twentieth-Century American West*, Hal Rothman discusses the abusive, and soul-sucking nature of tourism: "Tourism is the most colonial of colonial economies, not because of the sheer physical difficulty or the pain or humiliation intrinsic in its labor but because of its psychic and social impact on people and their places. Tourism and the social structure it provides transform locals into people who look like themselves but who act and believe differently as they learn to market their place and its, and their, identity" (1998, 11–12).

Winthrop is a scripted place—not only by tourism, but by notions of the American West perpetuated in popular culture. Assuming a western facade has not simply led to Winthrop's sacralization as a tourist attraction, but has set the town off on an institutionalized path of perpetually restoring itself as an image of the American West. The building structures and artifacts enshrined at the local museum are also the new designs and objects found in the streets and shops, as businesses mechanically reproduce the "sacred site" through postcards and souvenirs. As a tourist site, Winthrop's authenticity is therefore staged, which raises the question whether a tourist can actually have the "true" western experience the town claims it is providing. Dean MacCannell's (1976) look at staged tourist settings, which draws on Erving Goffman's notions of social life as split into back and front regions, is useful here. According to MacCannell, front regions are social areas that virtually mask the stable community, while back regions in one sense or another grant more access to the "real" people. Winthrop displays subtle gradations in the move from front to back. Recently constructed hotels and stores intended for tourists would, for example, be almost exclusively front regions, while the lobbies of Sun Mountain Lodge, the Mazama Country Inn, and the Freestone Inn, which are decorated with locally produced furniture and products, would be front regions with back-region elements. Back regions that open themselves to outsiders include Winthrop's "historical"—as in "old"—buildings, such as Miss Olivia Hall's Dress Shop (now the Topo Café, celebrating "Asian Vittles"), the Duck Brand Restaurant, and the Shafer Museum. For the community these places are local constants, but the tourist can also think of them as quaint additions to their western experience. Some traditional back regions, such as pack trips, have been modified to accommodate outsiders, but in ways that suggest access to the local community of wranglers and outfitters. And finally, there are back regions that tourists are never allowed into and that even some longtime residents still yearn to enter—most obviously, membership in the local Winthrop community, which only those already a part of it can grant. Enjoyed almost exclusively by descendants of Winthrop's pioneer families, such membership is based on a network of family and work relations that binds people inextricably together as "real" Winthrop citizens. According to Rothman:

> Locals must be what visitors want in order to feed and clothe themselves and their families, but they must guard themselves, their souls, and their places from people who less appreciate its special traits. They negotiate these boundaries, creating a series of boxes between themselves and visitors, rooms where locals

encourage visitors to feel that they have become of the place but where the locals also subtly guide visitors away from the essence of being local. (1998, 12)

With time, however, tourism tends to reshape all of these distinctions in its own image. The sanctification of Winthrop through imposed icons of the American West does reaffirm a tourist/resident distinction, but one that blurs as the economically driven local community continually seeks to modify its appearance to conform to visitor expectations. Daniel Boorstin has called those moments when outsiders first see what they expect to see "pseudo events," which he describes as "bland and unsurprising reproductions of what the image flooded tourist knew was there all the time." Such images must be "easily photographed (plenty of daylight) and inoffensive—suitable for family viewing." Above all, they must be familiar, because the tourist's "appetite for strangeness" is actually "best satisfied when the pictures in his own mind are verified in some far country" (1961, 109). As anyone familiar with the heated controversies over logging and endangered species in the Pacific Northwest already knows, the great forests are themselves increasingly becoming more pseudo-event than actuality. Sweeping along the North Cascades Highway, visitors may find their imaginations gratified by the vastness and beauty of the unbroken, magisterial forest on either side. In fact these trees are often screens, hiding from view acres of clear-cut wasteland beginning just yards from the road. And yet, "faux or real, scenery evokes powerful emotions" (Rothman 1998, 22).

As for Winthrop itself, with its picturesque facades and friendly—or sometimes authentically unfriendly—staff, businesses like Three-Finger Jacks, the Duck Brand Inn, Sheri's Sweet Shop, businesses located in the Purple Sage Building, the White Buck, and the Emporium have proved alluring for tourists. These businesses stay busy during holidays, Christmas break, and summer, when the town is choked with visitors. As a consequence of this success, however, gratified outsiders are investing more of their money and desires in the area, profoundly changing the community in the process. By 1994 Winthrop enjoyed the dubious distinction of having more espresso machines per capita than that renowned coffee town, Seattle. In addition, recreational tourism (which has become increasingly popular) such as cross-country skiing, snowmobiling, rock and mountain climbing, biking, hiking, river raft-

Main Street, Winthrop, Washington, 2005. Photograph courtesy of Karen Cowdrey

ing, and fishing have also become appealing local tourist activities, creating another subtext to an already complex tourist economy. Finally, more and more visitors have bought a piece of this rugged and beautiful mountainous region, creating a class of absentee landowners who pay for their relatively expensive homes by making them available for nightly rentals, bringing more strangers, and thus change, to the valley. Even those outsiders who leave their vacation homes empty have an effect. Year-round residents generally resent the idea of houses standing vacant when Winthrop's rental market is extremely tight and expensive. The legal westernization of Winthrop affects all residents of the Methow Valley as well as tourists, displacing everyone with the assumption of authenticity. Motivated by economic need, residents try to live up to notions of the American West, even though they might not necessarily identify with those cultural or political codes or are repelled by the social changes incurred by their community. Tourists who pay for "inclusion into a cultural myth" unknowingly also buy into a paradox, since there is "an equally strong cultural pattern of excluding the outsider" (Rothman 1998, 15).

As Bauman notes, although the "representation of cultural objectification is a complex ideological and political process," critics interested in the relationship of knowledge and power "have suggested that the power to represent or consume other cultures is a form of domination" (1986, 304). At least as far as their personal integrity is concerned, often Winthrop residents disagree. "I don't like to call it [Winthrop] a tourist attraction," says Kathryn Wagner, one of the original advocates for westernizing. "This is a living town. People live in it. They aren't tourist attractions" (Portman 1993, 173). And of course, the western tradition itself would lead us to expect that no matter how dependent they may now be on tourism for their survival, those who work with horses insist that true cowboy culture remains uncontaminated—a back region into which tourists may be invited, but which they cannot remake into their own image.

Cowboy/horsewoman work still requires physical strength; long experience and adeptness with those profoundly unpredictable animals, horses and mules; the ability to perform hundreds of different occupational tasks; and the judgment to deal instantly and effectively with dangerous situations. Other customs—from the setting down of a hat to more complex practices such as always giving the least experienced wrangler the rowdiest horse—are built on the work aspects of cowboy culture. Even cowboy poets, who travel about the United States reading their works, had better spend some time each year on a ranch if they want to retain their authenticity.

And as the cowboy poets themselves prove, the "relationship between verbal expression and cultural terminology" is one of the strongest indicators of how occupations "literally shape the cultural perspectives of their practitioners." And yet, despite Robert McCarl's optimistic view that "the unique occupational jargon or language within each trade" produces metaphors that "provide the folklorist with an appreciation of how the culture of work can be most successfully approached," at least in my experience, the fact of tourism inflects—and often in ways that can't be fully determined—even the language of working cowboys and horsewomen (1986, 76–77). Take, for example, the issue of accent. Since many people working with horses in Winthrop sound vaguely Texan, such an accent in horsewomen could presumably be explained as evidence of their status as authentic members of a working cowboy culture, and a quick return to my audiotapes at one point confirmed my impression that although none are from Texas,[1] most of my informants have "cowboy accents" to some degree. What I have realized, however, is that the degree might depend far more on tourism than on cowboy culture. One experience set this matter straight.

When my friend Cathy McCosham and I went riding with Kit McLean Cramer in the summer of 1995, Cathy, who is Canadian and who had ridden with Kit in 1994, asked me afterward if Kit had been to Texas (she had not), since her accent was heavier than the year before. The remark at least raised the possibility that Kit's western inflection might be more acute than the other horsewomen's because she works with more tourists on a daily basis and therefore has greater reason to display such an accent as proof of her professional authenticity. Listening to Marva Mountjoy's accent, shaped by her Basque origins in Idaho, become more distinct when telling stories to tourists or talking with them around campfires in the evening, only strengthened my suspicions. And Virginia Bennett, cowboy poet, who comes from New Hampshire, had a pronounced western/Texan voice that seemed to deepen as our interview progressed.

In these cases, however, the function of language, as both a claim of membership within a working culture and a performance designed to confirm the tourist's vision of authentic western experience, is to establish some form of community with each of the different audiences. When we turn our attention to jokes in a tourist environment, such assumptions fall apart, but in interesting ways. Both within and between groups, joking language proves to be far more complicated and even potentially divisive in its dynamics. McCarl, for example, notes that joking relationships often mirror "one's position in the canon of work technique" and that "a joke about technical ability is only permissible when one has an established reputation as an accomplished worker. If this individual was not accomplished or was considered incompetent, then a joke about the need for training wheels would be no joke at all, but a message designed to force the incompetent worker out of the group, or at least challenge his right to the job" (1986, 78–79).

One example of joking relationships between insiders and workers in cowboy culture is Lauralee Northcott's song "Yuppie Packer." A writer, musician, radio talk-show host, and third-grade teacher, Lauralee consented to be interviewed in 1999 and 2005 in her home. As was the case with the other women in this book, I had heard a lot about Lauralee beforehand and had seen her perform on two different occasions. She has lived in the Methow Valley for thirty years and married into a local pioneer family. At the time of our interviews she played in an all-girl trio, Horse Crazy, which performed "The Foggy Dew Western Review" for a variety show in Twisp, Washington, that she organized.[2] Lauralee's radio show "The Dollar Watch Cowboy Show" has been featured at the Academy of Western Artists and "gained national recognition through the web site 'Omar West's Cowboy Poetry at the Bar-D Ranch' (www. cowboypoetry.com)" (Gracie 2002, B6). On Sunday evenings Lauralee plays western music and reads cowboy poetry, and each week she invites someone from the community to tell a "true" story about the region or a tall tale. In March 2003 she released her third CD, *Car Tunes*. And she is currently working on another collection of western music.

Though busy, in the summer Lauralee often cooks for several different outfitters. She's a freelance cook, preferring to be available to all the outfit-

Horse Crazy in rehearsal: Lauralee Northcott, Emele Clothier, and
Virginia Bennett, 2000. Photograph courtesy of Karen Cowdrey

ters rather than working for just one. The Methow Valley outfitters like her, because she's a good cook and can sing and tell stories around the campfire. In the following song, Lauralee can make fun of the image of the cowboy or packer without diminishing him, as she is part of the Methow Valley and cowboy community. Her lifestyle, music, and writing are intricately involved in the perpetuation of the cowboy image. She often begins this song by explaining: "This one is called 'Yuppie Packer.' It's about going in the mountains and finding our packer on top of the Amphitheater with a cell phone, which we felt was pretty bad, that he had a cell phone up there. So we teased him about it. We teased him so long that I finally wrote this song."

Yuppie Packer

There was a young man, who had visions and dreams,
and he saw his life among the mountains and streams,
and he wanted to make his livin' in the hills,
And he knew he could handle the wrecks and the spills.
For he loved those moonlit nights out in the cold,
with those campfires that burned and stories of old,
he was a traditional man in the Western way,
but modern needs got in his way,
and he's a Yuppie Packer, can't leave his phone behind.
Yeah, he's a Yuppie Packer callin', from the peaks on the off-peak times.
He has to search for the highest spot and climb to the sun,
to get a clear connection on Cellular One.
He knows that business and romance are uncomfortable mates.
So he acts ignorant of software and long distance rates,
and he sneaks out of camp as quiet as a mouse,
and nobody knows he's called down to the house.
He reminds his wife who he is, hears all the latest news,
she recites his messages, he figures out all the business he will lose, and
    he muses how a laptop in his saddlebags might make life easier,
and he wonders if the information highway is the sickness or the cure.
Yeah, he's a Yuppie Packer and he really is cool.
Yeah, he's a Yuppie Packer, heck he's even been to school.

He's got a VISA card, got a MasterCard, even got an Eddie Bauer credit line,

and he might even buy stuff, if he only had the time.

Sometimes he worries about taxes as he is looking at the view.

Mr. Audit dogs his tracks as he spits another chew,

for how do you tell someone from Ogden, Utah,

that last hunting season was the last cash you saw. But tonight

    will find him listening for bells and snuggled up tight,

and he hopes those horses don't take it in their heads to travel tonight.

Yeah, he's livin' on the edge but he likes the company,

but he wonders if this Western education might be killing me.

Yeah, he's a Yuppie Packer, not gonna work harder, he's gonna work smart,

if he can only convince seven mules, every one an ornery old fart.

So I wish him the best and hope his batteries will last,

Till he passes the last crest on Robinson Pass. (1999)

Country music has always been a means for communicating values inherent in American culture, but—due in part to the 1980s political notions of Ronald Reagan and the "New Right"—country music has assumed a new popularity. In *Wanted Dead or Alive: The American West in Popular Culture*, Kenneth Bindas argues that "the New Right appealed to troubled Americans by advocating a return to rugged individualism and other traditional values associated with the West." Paradoxically, while maintaining notions of individuality and tradition, during the past twenty years country music has grown to reflect "conflicting images of the West" but has "also mirrored American's ambivalent attitudes towards gender, race, ethnicity and class" (1996, 232). In "Yuppie Packer" the lyrics reflect values implicit in cowboy culture and especially in relation to images of men and nature. But the song also suggests that images of the cowboy have been revised for twenty-first-century ideologies of gender and popular culture. The packer begins as an image of the American West: a cowboy who wrangled people as he embodied nature and the last frontier. Like tourists on his pack trip, the packer imagines himself fitting into an idealized wilderness scene: sleeping outside in the cold, relishing the warmth of the campfire, where he listens to or tells stories that just happen to reflect the cowboy images he projects for himself. A "traditional man in the Western way," the packer embodies the characteristics of the imagined cowboy serving as a symbol of individuality and competence. Beverly J. Stoeltje notes that in the myth of the West, the cowboy is "characterized by his horse, membership in an all-male group, alcohol (whiskey), loneliness, contact with the raw elements and animals, mobility, honor, sometimes a pistol, sometimes a fiddle" (1975, 27).

Up to this point in the song, the packer fits well with idealized images of western men. But when "modern needs got in the way," the image of the packer/cowboy begins to unravel. Though in camp and probably around the campfire with guests, he assumes the facade of ignorance regarding technology. This particular icon of American male independence begins to sneak away from camp to call home on his cell phone and "muses" to his wife "how a laptop in his saddlebags might make life easier." He is educated—a trait not usually associated with the cowboy—and he even worries about taxes in a middle-class and culturally mainstream way. The song ends in a blur of images that flip between the packer's real responsibilities, images of the cowboy, and implements of popular culture. Packers, for instance, often sleep near where the horses are pastured for the night. One horse or mule wears a large bell, so the packer can readily find the herd in the morning if it has wandered off. But this packer is stretching, in a way, since "he's livin' on the edge"—not necessarily an image that would spark confidence in the guests he is packing for. While a certain lack of confidence is reflected, he questions whether "this Western education might be killing me." According to Lauralee, this line is a direct reference to her, when her packer wondered out loud if life out on the trail was getting "a little Western on her," which meant out of control—like a horse or mule wreck (phone interview 2003). The songwriter is turning this metaphor back onto the packer, who even though "he's gonna work smart" still has "seven mules" to pack out of the wilderness—"every one an ornery old fart." And yet, though things seem to be getting "a little Western" on him, the song wishes the packer the best, with "hope his batteries will last / Till he passes that last crest on Robinson Pass." The song therefore does not end with a solid resolution, as the audience is left wondering whether the packer had a wreck, and if he did, whether he had enough battery power to call home.

Can a yuppie packer make it out alive in the American West? Yes and no, for according to Bindas, while "country music questioned the mythic West long before the 'new western history' ever did," it is also true that "consumers of the music have repeatedly demonstrated their preference for the mythic cowboy and West, even in the face of evidence that demonstrates that the West was made up of more than cool water, rye whiskey, and cowboys. To this day many country music consumers cling to the mythic West as the last refuge for American individualism" (1996, 236). The humor in "Yuppie Packer" therefore arises from a contemporary songwriter who daily makes connections with western culture. Lauralee's integration into the community is complete. She is accepted as a knowledgeable insider—someone allowed to joke about other insiders who stretch images of the American West, yet who waver on the edges of incompetence in reflecting that image.

When the "incompetent" is an outsider or tourist, the same joke can send exactly the opposite message, actually comforting or reassuring the target. This bifocal quality of joking language often parallels the horsewoman's bifurcated strategies, as she works overtly and covertly within the confines of the cowboy and tourist codes of the West, making her living not only by daily proving her professional expertise to her peers, but also validating the tourist's vivid fantasies about true encounters with the "real West." Not surprisingly, the horsewoman often turns to jokes as a way of sustaining herself in her work with horses.

On my three pack trips with Marva Mountjoy, I have been grateful for her expertise at handling horses and maintaining the camp and for her sense of humor. We were as safe and well cared for as we would have been on any vacation tour. It wasn't until later, when I heard the following stories, that I understood just how much ingenuity and downright misrepresentation packers often employ to sustain the western experience for their guests. Marva told me the story "Salting the Hole" in her kitchen, while making Basque bread for a pack trip leaving the next day for Spanish Camp in the Pasayten Wilderness. By way of background to the story, Claude Miller, her boss, had given Marva's name to another Methow Valley outfitter who was taking a group into the wilderness. His guests wanted to pan for gold, and since Marva and her husband have family mining claims in Idaho and were thus familiar with panning and mining techniques, Steve asked her to join the trip as camp cook and to teach everyone—including himself and the other packer—the finer points of panning for gold.

SALTING THE HOLE

These guests wanted to learn how to pan for gold. So the day before, I'd taken the packers, Steve and his friend, and we went back up to the creek where we were going to show the guests how to pan. I told them [the packers] what you had to do—that you had to block the water off in the creek. It was just a real hilarious thing because here are these cowboys in their chaps, boots, and spurs trying to be gold miners. So anyway, I had these guys blocking off the water with a manny.[3] We're all digging a hole in the creek and getting wet. We were getting the guests set up for the next day.

The next day the guests come up and I show them how to pan. And we're sitting in the creek and we're panning. Of course, we're not finding anything. I'm panning hard. Pretty soon I holler to Steve, "Could you come over and finish this pan? I'm just so stiff and tired; I can't sit in the creek any more. Just keep shaking it like this and doing like this and pretty soon, if you're lucky, you're gonna see some cube iron and little rubies. When you get it down even further, well, then you'll see some flecks of gold."

So Steve sits down in the creek and he's just panning away and he says, "God, Marva, is this what you're talking about? Cube iron?" He showed me his pan.

"Yeah," I said, "that's it."

And boy, the guests started to flock in now. Pretty soon there's lots of little rubies in the bottom of this pan. I mean, the guests are asking, "Where'd you get that, Marva? Which hole were you in?"

And they're [the guests] just all flocking. They're running to these holes, and filling their pans, and back out in the creek. They're just going crazy. Pretty soon, Steve's got the technique down. We can see the colors down in the bottom of the black sand. And I had kind of told him what to be looking for anyway. Pretty soon, I mean there's a dozen people. They're in the creek just a going crazy. I'm standing over Steve's shoulder and we're looking at the gold. Steve looks up at me and he finally realizes what I done.

"Thanks, Marva, I owe ya on this one."

Unbeknownst to our guests, of course, Marva had been to Silver City [Idaho] the week before and had saved all the gold that we had panned out in a mayonnaise jar.[4] So when I got to panning, I salted the holes. The guests never knew.

But by God, when they went home they had stories to tell. They had found their gold nuggets.

So maybe it's the things that go on behind that the guests aren't aware of. They never did know. They really thought I was a hero and that I knew how to pan for gold. I have no idea if there's gold up there or not! (1995)

At one time many gold and silver mines operated in the Winthrop area, so it is at least possible that some gold flake might have been in this stream. In any case, by expressing a desire to pan for gold the tourists had already made their request for a pseudoevent. The real story here, however, is a behind-the-scenes account of how Marva provides her guests with an apparently "authentic" experience.

To understand the dynamics of this story, a word or two about kinds of tourist experiences might be helpful. As Barbara Kirshenblatt-Gimblett explains, while tourist settings such as Disneyland "are blatantly contrived and accepted as such," others base their economy on offering the visitor access to authentic or true experience—real mountains instead of papier-mâché, real people instead of actors (1993, 304). As we've seen, though, tourists usually have a profoundly conditioned idea of what the reality of a place such as Winthrop will be. When a community commits itself to furnishing such pseudoevents for visitors, a self-sustaining circle of expectations between tourist and host soon comes to define their relationship. Valene Smith puts it this way: "If the economic goals of mass tourism are realized and the occasional visitor is replaced by a steady influx, individual guests' identities become obscured, and they are labeled tourists who, in turn, may be stereotyped into national character images" (1989, 14). Faced with what they see as indistinguishable visitors, all driven by the same expectations, the community predictably responds by mechanically reproducing what the stereotyped visitor wants. One experience fits all. Tourists thus cause their hosts to hold up a theatrical mask of sorts, to act as if "'onstage' when they meet in face to face encounters" (Nuñez 1989, 268). When I interviewed Ann Henry in 1999 (she cooked for Claude Miller for a number of years before retiring in 2002), she told me that she often "dressed up" for certain guests. Not in gear typical of the American West, but sometimes in a French maid's costume. Another time, when the theme was

Ann Henry (*left*) and guests, Hawaiian theme pack trip, 1999.
Photograph courtesy of Ann Henry

Hawaiian, packers and guests dressed up in aloha shirts and muumuus and wore plastic flowers. She called those trips "a lot of fun" (1999).[5]

Visitors respond in a number of ways to this situation. Some accept their hosts at face value, getting exactly what they want and are willing to pay for. For the community this kind of guest is the "tourist," a term MacCannell claims is "increasingly used as a derisive label for someone who seems content with his obviously inauthentic experiences" (1976, 94). As the word "seems" suggests, it should also be noted that the transaction itself denies visitors any other experience, for as "guests become dehumanized objects that are tolerated for economic gain, tourists have little alternative other than to look upon their hosts only with curiosity, and too, as objects" (Smith 1989, 14). The host-and-guest relationship represents a shared process by means of which tourist and host flatten out and objectify each other in an endless spiral of trivializing opposition. Aware that such dynamics do govern many tourist encounters, however, other visitors become so skeptical that "they may adopt an attitude of staging suspicion and deny the authenticity of sites that have not been staged" (Kirshenblatt-Gimblett 1993, 303).

Convinced that "authentic situations may be encountered by adventurous tourists who move off the beaten track," such visitors avoid the tourist traps on principle, convinced that "surprise" encounters will in some way be more "real" (Erik Cohen 1984, 375). Paradoxically, tourist economies respond to this inquiring attitude by providing a number of highly institutionalized services for gratifying it. Among these services is the tour, which "is characterized by social organization designed to reveal inner workings of a place; on tour, outsiders are allowed further in than regular patrons; children are permitted to enter bank vaults to see a million dollars, allowed to touch cows' udders, etc." As MacCannell goes on to note, however, within a short time "a staged quality to the proceedings" gives such tours "an aura of superficiality, albeit a superficiality not always perceived as such by the tourist, who is usually forgiving about these matters" (1976, 98). Put another way, then, the insiders' tour can be every bit as inauthentic as the standard experience. Lauralee Northcott recently imagined how tourists could experience authenticity with the residents of the Methow Valley. She was riding a bicycle back to her house while brainstorming a commercial for "The Dollar Watch Cowboy Show." She imagined a Web site entitled Dream Shack.com, "a realty company with an attitude":

> Are you looking for a place in the woods, an idyllic place, where the pipes freeze in the winter and you can't get any water in the summer? Where the pack rats give you visiting rights on the weekends? Yes, you too can own a place in the woods. Just come and visit us. Our virtual tour is at www.dreamshack.com. Prices starting at $500,000. (2005)

In the tourist economy of the Methow Valley, the pack trip seems to offer tourists their best chance for a real experience. Taking place in the wilderness, far from the manipulations of the tourist town or even the ranch, such a trip allows the discriminating visitor to escape for a time not only the stresses of home, but also the adulteration of "staged" tourist experience. But as "Salting the Hole" demonstrates, the wilderness pack trip can be as calculated and staged as any other guided tour. The logistics themselves suggest why, since the visitor who goes on an "authentic" pack trip usually pays for others to do all the "authentic" work involved and certainly pays for the expertise necessary to complete such a trip successfully. An outfitter must provide the horses, mules, and tack. The cook shops and packs the food in kitchen boxes, leads the trip down the trail, sets up the cook tent, cooks three meals a day, cleans it all up, and takes guests on day rides. And the packer serves as camp slave, packing all the gear onto the mules; saddling and unsaddling the horses, then feeding and grazing them; chopping wood, hauling water, digging the outhouse hole (often on precarious perches—another "inside" joke on the guests), then burying the deposits; building and maintaining the campfire; and sleeping with the horses at night. Small wonder, then, that even tourists "motivated by a desire to see life as it is really lived, even to get in with the natives," are still "depreciated for always failing to achieve these goals" by the very people paid to insure success (MacCannell 1976, 94).

The trip Marva describes in "Salting the Hole" would at first seem to be a classic example of how the yawning gap between resident and visitor can create humor. To begin with, there's the absurdity of the tourists' being so certain about what would make their pack trip "authentic" that the outfitter, who knows nothing about panning for gold, must find someone to teach him how to be an authentic gold-panning cowboy for his customers—an idea that Marva finds "real hilarious." Furthermore, although the visitors actually have their experience—Marva even refers to the prize as "their" gold nuggets—the whole adventure is a staged fraud. Or as Marva puts it, apart from what she adds to the river, she had "no idea if there's gold up there or not!" And finally, the guests are at times described in tourist stereotypes, "flocking" like birds to the hole and "just going crazy" when their fantasy is fulfilled. What makes this story especially interesting for my purposes, however, is its refusal to drop simply into the "greening the greenhorn" paradigm—and for intriguing reasons.[6] There's the remarkable generosity, for one thing. Although Steve is not even her regular employer, Marva takes the products of her own panning from the week before and salts the hole, apparently just for the simple pleasure of watching the tourists become ecstatic. You could perhaps argue that she is thinking about future business, and certainly these visitors will go back to their hometowns and rave about the gold to be found and the adventure to be had if you pack in with Steve and his crew. But there's no real suggestion that Marva ever considered repeating the practice. Then there's her careful shifting of the pan into Steve's hands, on the "feminine" grounds of stiffness and tiredness, which insures that the group's outfitter is the one who strikes gold.

Most fascinating of all is the way that Marva actually plays a joke on a cowboy and gets thanked for it. Steve is, of course, a "greenhorn" as far as panning is concerned, but Marva does trick her employer, and with tourists watching. The genius of the joke, however, which even Steve acknowledges, is that the tourists' desire for a pseudoevent keeps them from detecting both the fraud and Steve's gullibility. Even more impressively, Steve must also confess that Marva's joke has greatly enhanced his status with his customers. Falling for a woman's trick has paradoxically confirmed his authenticity as a cowboy. Here is horsewoman joking at its finest. For the tourists, Marva emerges as an authentic expert on gold panning; for her male peers, she must be recognized for her intelligence and professionalism ("Thanks, Marva, I owe ya on this one") even though in this story she displays these qualities to best advantage at the cowboy's expense. Marva ends her story by speculating that "maybe it's the things that go on behind that the guests aren't aware of" that really make the experience. But this conclusion does not lead to contempt for the visitors or, for that matter, Steve and other male employees. It is, after all, professionally gratifying for any horsewoman to know that guest and cowboy alike "really thought I was a hero and that I knew how to pan for gold."

This satisfaction and pleasure certainly came through in Marva's gregarious and animated telling of the story. One last note. When I asked her to explain what the term "salting the hole" meant, although she knew it referred to putting saltpeter in a mine hole to make it seem as though there were minerals in the area, she also offered an answer that neatly sums up this story and the general practice of a horsewoman's joking as well. "It means making something taste better," she said.

When I interviewed Shiril Cairns in 1992, she admitted, "These pack trips are a lot different—a lot different than the image you might take with

Marva Mountjoy and coffee on the kitchen box stove, 2000.
Photograph courtesy of Karen Cowdrey

you." Issues of the desire for an "authentic" tourist experience emerge in Shiril's anecdote:

I don't do any hunting trips. Well, I did do that for about a year—what a mistake. I decided to leave that one [kind of trip] to the established outfitters.

When a guy shows up to go on a pack trip and he's got double bandoleers with bullets across his chest—like this [she demonstrates] . . . you have an idea that this may be somebody who is a little [gestures—forefinger twirling at temple] . . . you know . . . when you spend $2,000 on a camouflage equipment?

I even had one guy that brought in a camouflage portapotty. He wouldn't go on [the high hunt] without his camouflage portapotty. So I tied it on the horse.

But he couldn't find it when he left—which I thought was great. So somewhere in these hills is a camouflage potty. You know, they even make camouflage toilet paper?

It's funny. Everyone [the hunters] takes all this stuff, but the guys never get out of their tents until nine—which is too late for their kill. But at nine, they get out and wander around in the same areas—shooting randomly. If there had been any game around, they'd be long gone.

The best thing for a hunter to do on a hunting trip is to come back to the campfire and drink. (1992)

Assuming the "tourist mask" is nowhere more evident than in the following anecdote told by Jessie Dice, with some assistance from her sister, Meghan Sullivan. Talented horsewomen, Jessie and Meghan inherited Rocking Horse Ranch from their mother, Shiril Cairns. I interviewed the two, good storytellers, in the ranch house where guests check in for rides. Most of the stories they told in some way incorporated their mother, who died of cancer in 1998. As Jessie and her mother discover in the story, a professional facade can sometimes be detrimental not only to the horsewoman, but to the livestock and the guests as well. Wanting a "real" horse experience can cross physical lines.

JESSIE: I just remembered my funniest moment. About four years ago, I took out a ride. This lady had called to make reservations for her and her sister about three months in advance. She said every year, they took

Shiril Cairns, 1990. Photograph courtesy of Jessie Dice and Meghan Sullivan

vacations together. They were both cello players but played in different orchestras. They called back several times to make sure the reservations were good. They seemed worried.

I pulled out some horses and had saddled one. We try not to saddle them until the riders are there just in case we have to change saddle sizes. Or sometimes there are more or less people. Whatever. You don't want horses standing there, in case the people are late—or they don't show.

So these ladies pull up in a red sports car and get out. Our jaws just drop. They are just huge. I mean huge—like 250 or 300 pounds—just huge women.

Mom said, "Oh, boy."

You know, she'd been talking to them. We try to have this policy, although it's difficult to do politely, about asking people their weight when they make reservations.

MEGHAN: But that's just recently.

JESSIE: Right. We made the policy because of this ride. Mom totally regretted not asking, because she'd been promising and promising the ride. "All right," she said.

We had two big horses. Mom went over and talked to the guests. "Have you guys ridden before?"

"Yes, we have," they said.

"Well," Mom said.

And they were just going on and on about how much they were looking forward to the ride. They just couldn't wait. They loved horses. They loved being out in nature. They loved empathizing with horses. They were really getting into it.

"All right," Mom said, "Jess, go."

We told them that the saddled horse had a bad foot. But really, he was too small. We took out our two biggest horses. We told them we had to take a shorter ride, for an hour. We came up with some excuse for the shorter ride. We were trying to be nice.

MEGHAN: We lie a lot in this business.

JESSIE: The people are important. You don't want to hurt their feelings by saying something like, "I'm sorry, you're too fat to ride." We got that from Mom. She had a hard time saying no.

MEGHAN: To anything.

JESSIE: To kids, people, horses, anything. Anything.

MEGHAN: We can't say no to anything.

JESSIE: Maybe that's women.

So we get out there and the horses did great. Shiloh, the big Appy, and Jodus, our big Paint. Jodus is the biggest horse we've got.

So we set off but we stayed totally flat. I wouldn't take them on any hills. I wouldn't let them trot. I'm just watching the horses the entire time. They were doing all right. I wouldn't let the riders get down—usually we let people get down halfway through to stretch their legs. I looked at them and thought, naw-ah—not this time.

So we're coming back down this county road over here and I notice that Shiloh's knees are starting to buckle. I said, "I think something's wrong with one of Shiloh's feet. You're going to have to get off." I knew Shiloh was going to lay down in a minute. I didn't want that lady's legs trapped underneath him. So I jump off my horse and go over and grab Shiloh's rein to help the lady get down. She says, "okay."

She leans over to swing her leg over the saddle. But she had to lean way far over cause of her big fat legs, which were real short. And she got her belt stuck on the saddle horn. So as she was sliding over the side, she started to slip down. She didn't realize her belt was stuck until she was on the side of the horse. She barely had one foot in the stirrup. Shiloh was starting to tilt over. I was trying to hold him up and he's falling over. I'm yelling, "Get your belt unstuck! Get your belt unstuck!"

She said, "I can't."

I had to get underneath her—her butt in my face. I had to get UNDERNEATH her to push her with my shoulder up far enough so she could get her belt off the saddle horn. She got it loose. I just stepped back. She just fell down to the ground.

"Are you okay?" I asked.

"I'm fine," she said.

Jessie Dice (*left*) and Meghan Sullivan (*right*) feeding horses, 2005.
Photograph courtesy of Leslie Lanthorn

I pretended to check Shiloh's feet. "We need to walk him. You need to walk for a little while."

We took a shortcut back across the field here. By the time we got back across, he was walking steady again. The lady was really uncomfortable walking—she didn't like that. I didn't want her to have to walk on back into the barnyard. I managed to get her back up. I don't know how I did it.

They loved their ride. They had a great time, even with that little mess up. They even called the next day for another ride.

Mom said, "Sorry, Shiloh started peeing blood. It was too much weight on his kidneys. We don't have horses that are big enough for you."

She finally had to say it. We couldn't be making excuses.

I was sorry for the ladies and the horses, because this whole ride these ladies are going on and on about much they loved horses. And I

was wondering, well if you love them so much how come you're tortur-
ing them with all that weight? (2000)

Jessie's story reveals the desire to fulfill a tourist fantasy strongly associated
with the American West. Even the largest people can have a horseback ride
and experience a little thrill. But Shiril, a kindhearted but outspoken horsewoman, was not one to keep back such information as that her horse was
"peeing blood" when the women asked for another ride. There are limits to
accommodating the cowboy dream.

At another interview Meghan told me a variation of this story:

> Alex—the old Appy that is always free grazing in the yard—was the one who
> used to get all the heavy people or fat ladies. This lady gets out of the car. God,
> she must have weighed a good 275 or 300 pounds. This was a BIG woman. Mom
> said later, "I looked at Alex and I swear I saw his lips move saying 'Don't even
> think about it—no way—I am not carrying her down the trail.'" (2000)

In the following narrative, "No Pork Chops," Marva Mountjoy describes
another two-tiered experience—one version performed for the guests and
another jokingly shared with coworkers. The major differences here are the far
more sustained and elaborate joking between staff members and the far greater
potential for embarrassment and disaster that drives Marva's improvisations.

No Pork Chops

Another time last summer, I was in the wilderness with a big group. We'd come
back to camp after a day ride and Anita, my assistant, and I were fussing around
the kitchen boxes. I was saying we'd have pork chops for dinner.

Anita says, "Marva, I don't see any pork chops."

"Oh, got to be pork chops in there," I said. "We have fourteen guests—of
course, we've got pork chops."

So we fiddle around and search. Pretty soon, I've two or three small things.
Pretty soon, Joe's gone through it and found things. I'm just going, "Jesus
Christ, there are NO pork chops in here; I'm short one night's meat. How am I
going to feed fourteen people?"

So, first of all, I swear the packers to secrecy that our guests are not going to know this. Joe volunteers to ride out. The trip is thirty or forty miles or something. It's just way too much for him to do in one day. I'm saying, "No, we can't do that."

Well, the other packer suggests that he could get grouse, because he's got his pistol. Well, grouse season doesn't open for three days. And, God, besides, the game warden's wife [Marva is married to the local game warden—now retired] cannot be sending the packer out to kill grouse three days early! So we better scratch that off. So I don't know. We just stewed and stewed over this.

So, that afternoon, we go to the lake to fish and one of the guests asks me if I want to fish.

"Fish, yeah. Oh, yes! Vince [a packer], wouldn't you like to fish?"

"Naw, I'm not real big on fish," he says.

I kicked Vince hard and said to the guest, "We'd love to fish." We went to the other end of the lake and caught everything we could. By the time we had finished up, the guests had finished up. I had enough fish that I could swing it if I fried up a few steaks—not all of them, but part of them. So that night, we had steak and fish.

I thought the next night we'd have the leftover steaks and we'd throw them into some kind of casserole. Anyway, we were scratching in those boxes like you can't believe. We were picking rice out of soup mixes in order to come up with enough. And it was all the little things that went around.

When we ride back from our day ride, I always holler at my packers to be sure and get the meat out and make the coffee when we get into camp. So I holler out, "Don't forget to pull the meat out!" I thought they were going to fall off their horses, because they knew we didn't have any meat to pull out.

We get into camp and I told Anita, "We're going to put it in a Dutch oven. Guests think food is wonderful in a Dutch oven [a cast-iron cooking pot usually set over a low fire or hot coals]. And we just winged it.

"What do you think, Anita? Should we put some green beans in this casserole? Doesn't that recipe we're following call for green beans?"

"Yes it did, Marva. Three cans. I got them right here."

"And, it called for four cans of cream of mushroom soup?" We went to putting this thing together.

Pretty soon, the packer comes in and says, "You know what? My mom makes a recipe just like this. It's really good. Only you know, the darnedest is that she usually uses pork chops instead."

Our guests never knew. We fed them, but we did laugh at their expense. (1995)

A highly regarded "developmental tool, particularly for underdeveloped areas worldwide and even for rural districts of the United States," tourism can offer substantial economic benefits to a community by creating jobs and increasing cash flow. To the host population, though, tourism is often a mixed blessing. The work itself is labor intensive and frequently stressful, since the tourists can become a physical as well as a social burden, especially as their numbers increase. In "Tourist Studies in Anthropological Perspective," Theron Nuñez identifies two types of host individuals: those with prestige in their community, who may support a gradual increase in tourism, but not at the expense of their own authority; and those who are culturally marginal in some way, who see tourism as a means for rapidly changing their own social position.[7] Nuñez claims that the second group's partially alienated status makes its members ideal mediators between worlds, or "cultural brokers." He says "the marginal individual turns his/her marginality to their advantage and through entrepreneurship may be more adaptive than traditional economic subsistence pursuits. The marginal individual may be inclined/motivated to cope with the anxieties of tourism creatively" (1989, 268). Nuñez's notion of "host individuals" would place Marva in the latter category, as she is a relative newcomer to the valley—she's lived in Winthrop for only thirty years. She is also marginalized by the guests as "servant" and by her own community by gender. But she also displays versatility that is the result of her marginalization, which grants her an adaptability that the cowboys here clearly lack. In "No Pork Chops" Marva shows just how adaptive and creative she can be, not only by successfully maintaining the western illusion for her guests, but by staging a parallel comic performance for her own staff. The elaborate, multipart joke is born out of necessity: Marva is short a night's meat. Rather than letting her guests know that the western tradition of foresight and competence has been violated, however, she commits herself to a charade and makes the other packers swear to keep silent.

What follows is a story laced through with irony, which also paradoxically proves that Marva is a resourceful and imaginative wilderness professional. After ruling out an emergency trip for meat—it's far too long, won't be in time, and presumably might raise questions—Marva also rules out the desperate suggestion of killing grouse with a pistol. Instead she decides to play by the current wilderness rules and regulations. What's important for the story is that Marva is not only in charge, but she rejects two suggestions from male packers as impractical or even illegal solutions to their problems. Men try to offer help but prove unequal to the task. Nor does Marva come up with a solution that silences the other packers. Rather, she essentially asks her staff to trust her improvisational skills and to back her up on whatever she might do. Justification for such trust appears almost immediately. When the guests ask Marva if she'd like to fish, she pounces immediately on the possibility. Here the joke is twofold. First, the guests themselves are laughed at for unknowingly providing Marva with the means for keeping them in the dark. But second, Vince (the packer) is teased for being too dense to see how this moment might offer a way out of their food problem. Here Marva is definitely acting as a "culture broker," for it's obvious that without her there's no way that the charade could be maintained.

What happens next, however, reveals that another aspect of the tourist/ resident dynamic has come into play. As women in a male profession, horsewomen such as Marva must inevitably assume the role of marginalized innovator, as in both "Salting the Hole" and "No Pork Chops." Marva plays the part very well. But as Nuñez points out, the very act of working in the visitor industry can force people to construct a "tourist mask." This "mask" is a grotesque version of authenticity, a prop for a role "designed to accommodate tourists" (1989, 210). Furthermore, "performance is usually exaggerated before an audience of strangers": a working professional such as Marva, for instance, self-consciously presents herself as the archetypal horsewoman. Two consequences emerge from this fact, and both are found in "No Pork Chops." First, as she improvises, Marva finds her best tools for hiding the truth are those central to tourism itself. As MacCannell explains: "A mere experience may be mystified, but a tourist experience is always mystified. The lie contained in the tourist experience, moreover, presents itself as a truthful revelation, as a vehicle that carries the onlooker behind false fronts into reality" (1976, 103). Despite MacCannell's thundering disapproval—he states that the "touristic experience" is "morally inferior to mere experience" and that the whole process is "insidious and dangerous"—his remark that "an inauthentic demystification of social life is not merely a lie but a super lie, the kind that drips with sincerity" certainly helps to make sense of how Marva carries out her plan.

For what soon happens is that she starts putting on a performance that calls her peers' attention to the subterfuge by virtually taunting the tourists for their obliviousness. Yelling, "Don't forget to pull the meat out!" almost jolts the packers off their horses, because they can't believe Marva is calling attention to the meal. Then her improvising leads to the Dutch oven plan, in which Marva uses an "authentic" western cooking tool to make the tourists excited about what is actually a haphazard dish of what's available. At this point Marva starts conducting a class in the joys of telling such a superlie. By referring to a nonexistent recipe, Marva invites Anita into the game, and perhaps significantly, the other working woman catches on far more quickly than Vince did. But even the males finally join in, as the one packer brings the joke to a close by looking at the casserole, calling everyone's attention to the fact that there are no pork chops, and getting away with it. While he does have the punch line, he has to be educated by the situation's inherent humor to be able to deliver it.

This instruction in shared humor is Marva's response to the second consequence of assuming the "tourist mask." As Nuñez observes, when dealing with tourists, most hosts find themselves assuming roles "that they would never play before their peers" (1989, 268). Nothing, for instance, would undercut a cowboy's authority with others in his community more than an apparent pandering to tourists' notions of the West. In "No Pork Chops," however, Marva's success depends primarily on playing the western horsewoman role as broadly and confidently as possible while defusing any criticism or ridicule from the other packers by assigning them roles in the performance. Unlike "Salting the Hole," then, "No Pork Chops" shows how humor in the tourist environment can also be a powerful tool for erasing internal conflicts by establishing a tourist victim who can serve as a source of income and a butt for endless mockery. Or as Marva puts it, "Our guests never knew. We fed them but did we laugh at their expense."

There is no harm or malice in the humor of Lauralee, Ann, Marva, Jessie, Meghan, or Shiril. Like all the horsewomen in this book, they situate themselves within the dynamics of a male/female, insider/outsider, professional/greenhorn, resident/tourist, and subject/interviewee type of role. In difficult circumstances in the middle of the wilderness, they demonstrate an expertise in the hospitality business. The fact of the matter is that tourism plays an essential role in the identity of Winthrop and the Methow Valley. As an industry, tourism has become one of the largest economic factors in the world. Elke Dettmer notes that "tourism serves deep-seated needs of industrial urban people," but she points to the result that tourist interactions "have changed folk cultures more profoundly than any revolution or ideology" (1994, 187). As Winthrop's booming construction industry focuses on tourist accommodations and homes for absentee landowners, the face of the town, and of the townspeople, is increasingly taking on the features of the "tourist mask." As the stories in this chapter suggest, however, even the same horsewoman's attitudes, behavior, and performance will subtly shift depending on audience, companions, and situation.

CHAPTER TWO

A Woman's Code of the West

In *The Cowgirls,* Roach celebrates the American horsewoman's trailblazing feminist spirit. According to Roach, "the emancipation of women may have begun, not with the vote, nor in the cities where women marched and carried signs and protested but rather when they mounted a good cow horse and realized how different and fine the view" (1990, xxi). And yet, though horsewomen across the United States have for years been assuming active roles in a predominantly masculine arena and though many of their stories certainly reject sexual oppression and frequently seem to harbor feminist sentiments, these women often refuse to call themselves or to have others call them feminists. In her work on *Cowgirls,* a 2002 film documentary focusing on female rodeo riders in Calgary, Canada, Sally Clark found a similar political thread. When asked for her opinions about feminists, Milly Pedersen, a seventy-nine-year-old barrel racer, quipped: "If, by feminist, you mean the ones yelling for equal rights, I have no time or sympathy for them" (Bergman 2002, 52). When Burbick pursued interviews with former Lewiston, Idaho, rodeo queens, she was asked not to "Betty Friedan" her research. Burbick marveled at "how the author of *The Feminine Mystique* could have ended up as a verb, and a cautionary one at that" (2002, 7).

Issues of feminism often emerge in my college classes. As an assistant professor at the University of Hawaiʻi at Manoa, each semester I see how the definitions of feminism and gender politics are sublimated and distorted in popular culture. For example, in my freshman composition classes, students interview me on the first day. Then, based on the answers, students write a short biographical essay. One of the first questions is always whether or not I am a feminist. Even when I have tried to trick new students by wearing different costumes, such as a frilly pink dress and heels to display my femininity, the question is asked, often couched with fear, as if I could be some kind of feminist raptor ready to emasculate the male students and convert the females to my deadly politics. Actually, I find the question humorous as the attitude is so predictable and yet disturbing because the politics of gender evokes such concern. In class we discuss the basic premises of feminism, often with students agreeing to these ideas but then absolutely denying any association with feminism. It is okay if I am a feminist, perhaps because I am older and an academic, as long as I don't shove my beliefs down their throats. Embracing stereotypic images of the strident and probably lesbian feminist to varying degrees, the western women I interviewed often said that the term reflected negatively on them. "I'm not a woman's libber," Kit McLean Cramer responded when I asked about her notions of feminism; "I very much enjoy being a woman" (1995). Still, while appreciating the distance the horsewomen would like to keep from the cultural politics of feminism, I can only report that their lifestyles and stories often embody fundamental feminist assumptions.

Similarly surprising contrasts crop up when any aspect of the American horsewoman/cowgirl is examined. Before beginning my research, for instance, I assumed that except for perhaps a few isolated survivors, cowgirls were figures of the past. In fact, from pioneer days to today, many working horsewomen have been riding astride, roping, branding, and castrating steers throughout the rural United States.[1] And yet, because they seem to be invading a traditionally male domain, horsewomen have either been ingested or remain marginalized by the language, folklore, and humor of American cowboy culture. While stories, poems, songs, oral narratives, literary criticism, films, and television sustain the cowboy's mythic status as the epitome of self-reliance and individuality, there are few heroic or even notable western female role models.

Kristin M. McAndrews tying up Widow Maker, 2005.
Photograph courtesy of Karen Cowdrey

In the history, fiction, and film of the American West, male heroes abound. Historical figures such as Wyatt Earp, "Wild Bill" Hickok, Sitting Bull, and Crazy Horse as well as fictional characters such as the Virginian, Maverick, and Matt Dillon compose the male-dominant frame of the American West. In folklore and literature a plethora of scholarship exists on the cowboy hero and his contribution to images of the American West. But where is the research on cowgirls, the cowboy's female counterparts? While female rodeo riders such as Lucille Mullhall, Tad Lucas, and Alice and Margie Greenborough gained renown as exceptional athletes, more often than not in historic or fictional venues heroic western women appear to be cultural anomalies, such as Calamity Jane, Belle Starr, or Annie Oakley (LeCompte 1993, 28). Scholars of women in the West have noted not only the depiction of women as peculiar oddities, but also the absence of significant academic and cultural research concerning them. Jordon describes why some "quirky" women receive more press than others, explaining that Calamity Jane and Belle Starr "actively sought notoriety; it assured the place they had found for themselves as novel renegades, forever on the fringes of society. And if they led exciting, romantic lives, they still had about them the aspect of the clown or sideshow freak—something most women, with at least some inbred sense of social propriety, hardly cared to emulate" (1984, 276). Annie Oakley, referred to as "little sure shot" by Sitting Bull, was a persona created out of a Wild West show (Russell 1970, 21–25). In the imagery of the American West, the cowgirl's cultural roles are generally idiosyncratic, particularly because they cross gender lines. Cowgirls or horsewomen function as complex sociological phenomena reflecting and deflecting stereotypes of the American cowboy and standards of female domesticity. This shifting between norms has led to a kind of cultural invisibility.

Possibly this lack stems in part from the way that heroic folktale motifs are themselves gendered. In literature and folktales, male and female characters commonly pursue distinctly different quests. Acting alone, the male hero usually searches some uncharted physical terrain for an allusive object, which he eventually finds and brings back to his community. Both the object and his own enhanced knowledge enrich this society, for his success depends upon his ability to ask questions while questing and later to relate his adventures to his community. Self-reliant and strong, the male hero stands out in a crowd—the lonesome cowboy, if you will—but he must also make his achievements known. He is an educator/newsman/self-promoter of sorts. Women are different. In a folktale, when a female hero leaves her home it is usually because mistreatment or poverty forces her to do so or because she seeks to help endangered others. Although part of her heroic quest can turn out to be a sexual experience, she's not allowed to question her challenge in advance. In addition, commonly a male figure, either looming peripherally or physically present, is an essential participant in any successful female-hero quest. And finally, in folktales the female hero's adventure often takes place, and eventually ends, in silence. Either she dies in her quest for knowledge, or she returns to her community and mutely disappears into the marriage that is her reward.[2]

Of course women have been heroic on more diverse levels than the above folkloric description, but as a culture we cling to the social implications and comfort of folk narrative patterns that unconsciously reinforce cultural expectations of men and women. These motifs help make "sense" of our world; thus, images of women as significant heroic contributors to the cultural landscape tend to dissolve. And women's verbal contribution toward an understanding of cultural norms is markedly suppressed.

These points are especially evident when one examines images of women in the American West. In fact, it is a critical commonplace that images of the American West promulgated by literature and art tend to flatten or exclude women. "Although the 'good' women of the West—presumably white, married, middle-class pioneers—received a sort of obligatory nod in the western scenario," Anne M. Butler writes, "their status could be truly clarified only if they appeared in contrast to the 'bad' women of the West." For this reason, women like "the mule skinner Calamity Jane, the bandit Belle Starr and the sharpshooter Annie Oakley" have traditionally been dismissed "as the quirky exceptions that affirmed the maleness of western society" (1994, 776). Two points should be made about this practice. First, even within this framework, there were and are far more idiosyncratic females than western history, literature, and art have suggested. And second, the vast majority of these women are peculiar and quirky only in the minds of male-dominant culture, which has a long and distinguished tradition of imposing stereotypes on the spheres of influence that women have occupied, but which men know little or nothing about.

One might consider, for example, how seldom women resort to violence in the folklore and fiction of the American West. Toting guns and instituting gunplay is, of course, presented as the prerogative of men, while women appear as socialized towards passivity, making any physical or intellectual aggressiveness not just unacceptable but perverse. What further complicates this opposition, however, is the value placed on violence within western folklore and fiction. American history and literature tend to represent male power as the force of progress. As a result women's supposed nonviolence makes them insignificant, inarticulate, and unrecorded participants in the dominant culture's discourse of achievement.[3] Another way in which women have been written into, yet simultaneously out of, cowboy culture is their representation

Kelsey Gray riding near Shafer Meadow, 2005.
Photograph courtesy of Kit McLean Cramer

as being in need of male protection. As David Dary explains, "womanhood on the open range was placed in high esteem because there were so few women at first," but this "esteem" grew largely out of a recognition of weakness and vulnerability. Consequently, "a cowboy was to respect good decent women and protect their character" (1989, 279). Within the Code of the West, then, the cowboy's role was to take any insult against a woman personally and thus to react violently against the male transgressor. In fact, when women are written into cowboy culture, they are presented primarily as figures who allow and justify the exercise of male violence.

The consequences of this ethos for women are predictable, but they should be stated. Since within this framework they must rely on patriarchal culture for protection, women are also expected to remain passive when transgressions are committed against them. They have, in short, been socialized to fear men, which not only creates a population of potential victims of violence, but also paradoxically creates and sustains the male role of protector. As Annette Kolodny notes, such dynamics are often the most powerful determining forces in our narratives:

> Certain power relations, usually those in which males wield various forms of influence over females, are inscribed in the texts that we have inherited, not merely as subject matter, but as the unquestioned, often unacknowledged *given* of the culture. Even more important than the new interpretations of individual texts is the probing into the consequences (for women) of the conventions that inform those texts. (1985, 146–47)

To show how Kolodny's call for exploring the consequences of conventions would affect a reading of the West, one might look at the emblematic and practical relationship between western women and horses. As long as pioneering women have been present in the American West, they have been actively and necessarily involved in riding, roping, and branding cattle, helping their husbands work the range as well as maintaining the domestic life of the ranch. Within popular culture, though, riding a horse is virtually the same as being male, and because all common activities are related to it, the result has been twofold: a polite silence, which makes the horse-riding woman almost invisible; and, more strikingly, a repertoire of cultural practices that changes the significance of women's riding when it does take place. One way of displacing the significance and power of women's riding is to suggest it is sexual in nature.

Surprisingly, when I began my research into women's horseback riding, I had a few acquaintances suggest that there was something highly sexual about woman sitting on a horse, in a sort of self-gratifying way. These were well-educated, seemingly emancipated men, certainly aware of the cultural influences that shape gender. But still . . . the fantasy lives on.

An example of subsuming the import of women's riding was the sidesaddle, which was mandated for women until late in the nineteenth century. Jack Weston says, "If ever there was a contraption designed to keep women inactive, immobile, restricted in range and movement, helpless and demure, it was the sidesaddle" (1985, 169). Though uncomfortable and dangerous, the sidesaddle prevailed because as weaker, passive beings, women were assumed to have delicate legs, frail backs, and thighs too weak to grip the horse. Furthermore, as Susan Brownmiller notes, it was thought that "sustained bumping on the groin was not only indelicate," but "might be injurious" (1984, 190). Riding sidesaddle also sustained an extremely gendered notion of beauty. Straddling a horse not only might make a woman's buttocks appear too large, but would even make it possible for her, especially if she was a good rider, to be mistaken at a distance for a man. Sitting sideways prevented such problems, for it gave a woman a more vulnerable, crippled appearance—the mermaid look—which, as Brownmiller points out, has a great deal to do with the socializing of women's sexuality. Then as now, public female leg spreading is seen as loose, gauche, and immoral, traits "that the feminine woman must try and avoid, even as she must try to hint that somewhere within her repertoire such possibilities exist" (1984, 180). Except, of course, for sexual intercourse of a sanctioned kind, as women we must keep our legs firmly together, no matter how uncomfortable or impractical it might be.[4] "Initiative is the issue," Brownmiller contends, "and the feminine code of movement is designed to inhibit the thought. . . . The ideology of feminine sexual passivity relies upon a pair of closed thighs more intently than it does upon speculative theories of the effects of testosterone on the libido, aggression and the human brain. Open thighs acknowledge female sexuality as a positive, assertive force—a force that is capable of making demands to achieve satisfaction" (1984, 189).

My socialization certainly confirms Brownmiller's analysis. As a child, if my mother caught me sitting with my legs apart, she would first tell me that good girls did not sit like that and then darkly ask if I really wanted boys to see my underpants. A female student recently recalled that her father advised she should sit at all times as if she was holding an aspirin between her knees. As was the case for my student, social deviance and privacy violated by the male gaze were inevitable with spread legs. Even now, as a fifty-four-year-old with pants on, I'm still not comfortable sitting with my legs open. Except, of course, on horses, and I suspect part of the joy I receive from horseback riding results from the feeling that at some level I am disobeying some basic rules of feminine gentility. I become a cultural outlaw. I am tall. I am powerful.

That such clusters of socially gendered assumptions pervade the area of the West that I researched became clear when I interviewed an eighty-year-old resident of Omak, Washington, who had been an avid horseback rider as a young girl. Born and raised in Mazama, Washington, she told me that her father had put her bareback on their horse Blackie when she was four years old. Loving the work on horses, she was her father's cowhand and wrangler until she turned twelve, when her older brother, who didn't like working with horses and cows, was actually forced to take over her job. She was deeply confused as to why she could no longer ride with her father, but her mother explained that now she must learn other chores. "I never did have time [to ride] again until my kids were grown," she recalled. "I figured out later it was because I started my period" (1994). Apparently, then, with menstruation came sexuality; and with sexuality came gendered prohibitions that confine sexuality to certain limits. These restrictions not only concern horses and spread legs, but also significantly involve the work assigned highest status in the American West.

And yet, even when hampered by sidesaddles, babies, and rigid gender rules that proscribe as ungenteel not only chewing tobacco, spitting, and cursing, but also riding, working, and asserting themselves as long as they have been present in the American West, women nevertheless have lived and worked in those wilderness settings and frontier towns that supposedly created the necessary cultural conditions for literature and folklore in the American West.

Like most American females, when they entered the supposedly uncivilized and certainly male-dominated physical terrain of the wilderness, western women functioned as the traditional civilizers by raising families and contributing socially and economically toward the building of a community.[5] Scholars such as Stoeltje credit women with bringing institutionalized civilization to the wilderness: "Though the forms of institutionalization were skeletal—social occasions, funerals, religious instruction and the like—many participants and observers recognized that women assumed the responsibility for them. Their roles became established within the new environment, and values and emotions were expected to conform to these roles." Stoeltje argues that an "interaction between the demanding physical environment, and the social environment" produced "a modified image of women" (1975, 26), but for the most part this interaction has remained more of a felt opposition.

The resistance to women's pursuing a profession in a predominantly male territory often leads them to take on characteristics from both sides of this conflict. To do the physical work, horsewomen must be as strong as the men, but they must also behave in a ladylike manner. Complicating matters further is the fact that packing is now almost entirely a part of the hospitality business—which would in itself seem to be a "female" profession.

All of these tensions and demands are apparent in the way that Winthrop horsewomen deal with language. Although more has probably been written about the cowboy than any other American cultural figure, the cowboy is usually thought to be distrustful of words.[6] As a man of action, he would rather respond physically to a situation than talk his way out of it. Silence is a value of the Western. Cowboy heroes tend to grunt rather than talk, and when they do speak, it is in short, clipped sentences, ordering rather than expressing emotion. Men who talk too much or try to analyze a dangerous situation are seen as weak. In "Women and the Language of Men," Tompkins argues that in the Western, the strongest shaping force on the popular American image of the cowboy, "language is gratuitous at best; at worst it is deceptive" (1993b, 47). And often the deceivers are women, who, by talking too much, cast shadows into a world of emotional and ethical black and white. In the traditional Western, then, marginalized characters, not the cowboy hero, think with their mouths and get into trouble because of it.

Part of this admiration for straight talk or silence comes from another component of the western myth: the fundamental relationship between Man and Nature. Nature is bigger, more powerful, than any single person; in fact, its awesome vastness renders all human practices or beliefs somehow insignificant or pathetic. A kind of chivalry pervades the western male self-image, for it demands humility in the face of nature but celebrates personal strength, duty, and thoughtfulness when dealing with such weaker beings as women, children, and the defenseless.

As Babe Montgomery stated during one of our interviews, however, this same chivalry is also a thinly disguised strategy for asserting the male's innate

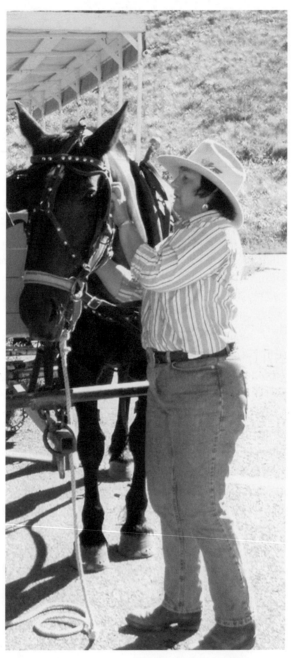

Lynn Breaky-Clark hitching draft horses for a wagon ride, 2005.
Photograph courtesy of Kristin M. McAndrews

superiority and making females feel weak and dependent, despite nature's own evidence to the contrary:

> I mean, these are the things that I have a strong antagonism with, what men do to women and the fact that women are so, what do ya call it, they're brainwashed, really, and have been brainwashed for many hundreds and hundreds of years into believing that the man is the master. Well that's foolish, 'cause in the wild the female has to be the one that uses the brainwork to keep the species alive. It isn't the male. The male just screws and goes on about his business, but the female is the one who keeps the species alive; and that's true in all of 'em. So the human race, the females of it, have let the men beat them to death and beat them into submission and coerced them. Women feel they have to perform and they've always been told that you're not much if you can't get a man. (1994)

Though she believes herself to be emancipated from this oppression—she says she quit looking for a man in her thirties—this horsewoman strongly believes that due to coercion, women in our culture have themselves come to accept the idea that they are not worth much if they are unattached to men. More specifically, her account of nature also calls into question one of the fundamental assumptions underlying male privilege. If, in fact, the female of the species doesn't need a man except for procreation, and if she is the fully functioning and intelligent inhabitant of the wilderness, then domestic culture not only denies women's strengths, but expects women themselves to uphold and nurture the frame of civilized repression, which excludes them from the male role of protector and leader.

Despite these cultural challenges, it is nevertheless true that often women's humor reflects an aggressive and physical attitude toward the very community that has sought to contain it. These associations between humor, aggression, and unfeminine behavior may help to account for the scarcity of critical work on women's place within humor studies, at least when compared to the richness of similar work on men.

Many theorists of gender and humor pay close attention to the implications and possibilities of a systematic and formulaic gender behavior, especially in relationship to language. Nina Auerbach argues that "all true communities are knit together by their codes," which "can range from dogmas to a flexible, private and often semi-conscious set of beliefs" (1978, 8–9). Elaborating on this idea, Joan Radner explains how coding within a community is not only multiple and multiform, but frequently exclusionary and even a subterfuge:

> We are not using code simply to designate the system of language rules through which communication is possible; in this sense any message is "in code." Rather, we mean a set of signals—words, forms, behaviors, and signifiers of some kind—that protect the creator from the consequences of openly express-ing particular messages. Coding occurs in the context of complex audiences in which some members may be competent and willing to decode the message, but others are not. (1993, 3)

For women and their stories, this state of affairs is both repressive and empow-ering. Auerbach notes, "in literature at least, male communities tend to live by a code in its most explicit, formulated, and inspirational sense" and, in the act of living, devote a great deal of energy to reinforcing this code as the culture's standard for meaning and value. In the face of such imposed authority, "in female communities, the code seems a whispered and a fleeting thing, more a buried language than a rallying cry" (1978, 8–9).

Making a virtue of this hard necessity, Radner extends Auerbach's account by suggesting that within such a dynamic, only those who are excluded or sub-ordinated can develop any real facility or versatility in their communications:

> Coding presumes an audience in which one group of receivers is "monocul-tural" and thus assumes that its own interpretation of messages is the only one possible, while the second group, living in two cultures, may recognize a dou-ble message—which also requires recognizing that some form of coding has taken place. Coding then is the expression or transmission of messages poten-tially accessible to a (bicultural) community under the very eyes of a dominant community for whom these same messages are either inaccessible or inadmis-sible. (1993, 3)

Even the most cynical horsewomen in the Methow Valley recognize the dis-tance between their assigned social role as women and their own perceptions of female identity. Although Babe Montgomery, for instance, lays much of the blame on women themselves for their submissiveness to males and their codes, by disgustedly observing that "women feel they have to perform," she suggests that a different set of assumptions lies behind even the most obedient performance of the conventional female role.

And frequently, it is in jokes that such sets of assumptions find their voice. Nancy Walker cogently describes how humor often articulates not just the dominant, but the subordinate codes of a community as well. As one of the expressions of the codes by which a group functions, humor's "topics and forms" provide "an index to the values and the taboos of the group, and the humor can be so intimately tied to group identity as to be almost unintelligible to anyone outside the group" (1988, 105–6). What complicates matters for horsewomen in the Methow Valley, however, is that they occupy two subordinate positions—one in relation to males in their own community, but another, which they share with these males, in relation to the outside tourist community that provides Winthrop men and women with their livelihoods. As I mentioned earlier, humorous tales that put the newcomer—the dude— off balance in an unfamiliar environment are in part a coded response to what John O. West describes as a sense of impotence and inferiority. Thanks to the economics of the situation, "the cowboy often had occasion to feel that tourists considered him to be an object for gawking at, ordering around, and treating like a monkey in a cage." Cowboys took their revenge in finding ways "to scare tourists into seventeen kinds of fits" (1990, 50).

At least in the area of mocking their source of income, horsewomen often join Winthrop males in upholding a tourist Code of the West. Within western culture, when women are not keeping their mouths shut, they are assumed to be using words primarily as a medium for expressing emotion—a form of discourse the dominant culture may appreciate at times, but which it certainly does not respect. Consequently, when a woman enters a professional realm that males consider their own, she finds herself both included and excluded from the Code of the West. Because she is more, she is also less.

In 1994 I interviewed Babe Montgomery on two separate occasions. Several women whom I spoke with in 1992 had recommended Babe as a must interview. When I asked why she was so important, the most common answer was that she was a real cowgirl and a *real* character. When I asked for further explanations, I was usually told about the time she rode her horse into Three

Finger Jack's in Winthrop and whipped the snot out of her first husband [Babe told me that it was actually the Road House Restaurant in Twisp, Washington]. Someone also told me about a time that she danced up on a piano at Jack's just to make her husband angry. But most of the people who knew Babe didn't want to spread gossip about her or say anything negative. She was well respected and revered as an expert horsewoman.

Knowing that she lived in Twisp, Washington, I sent three query letters to her through the Twisp post office, care of general delivery, regarding a possible interview. I received one reply in which she congratulated me on my pursuit of "word study." With the note she sent me a copy of an editorial she had written for the *Methow Valley News*. She claimed to have little time available but said to check in on her if I really wanted an interview. She gave me no phone number or address. When I arrived in the Methow Valley that summer, I spoke to workers at the senior center and the local library. While people knew who she was, they were vague about how I could find her. Finally, I asked the checker at Hank's Harvest Foods in Twisp, who told me that Babe came in most afternoons for lunch at the store deli. The checker described Babe as elderly and small. She typically wore a huge hat that looked like a combination sunbonnet and baseball cap. At lunchtime, wearing the large blue hat, she walked in. After all the stories I had heard, I assumed she had some girth about her, but she was tiny—about five feet tall—thin, slightly stooped, with her shoulder-length white hair tucked roughly into her hat. She pushed the door open with authority and took long strides with her short legs. I introduced myself. She acknowledged that she had received my letters but said she had not answered the first two because she was too busy to be interviewed. She told me that many people had wanted to interview her, but she wouldn't be interviewed by just anybody because that took time—which she didn't have. She directed me toward a small booth at the deli. "So tell me why I should spend my time talkin' to you?"

It was a good question. At that point I was still unclear about exactly whom and what I was going to focus on for this project. I knew from other women who lived in the valley that Ms. Montgomery was one cowgirl I needed to interview, but I still did not have a definitive direction for my project. I told her I wanted to write a book regarding women's humor in the American West. She

Babe Montgomery in her living room, 1994.
Photograph courtesy of Kristin M. McAndrews

laughed and suggested that not many women had a sense of humor. After a bowl of soup and a roll, she said she would have time to talk to me if I wanted to come out to her place and help out with her horses. I followed her truck back to her house near the old Twisp airport.

The small, run-down house was at the end of a road with no running water and a huge hole in the kitchen floor. She reminded me again that she had chores to do but agreed to sit and talk in her small living room. She had to bring her horses down from a pasture up the road. As she guided me in through the back door, she said she had better things to do than cleaning up, because she had horses to take care of, water to haul, and reading to do. The house was full of newspapers, empty dog-food bags, cats, mail, catalogs, and stacks of books. For the next hour we talked. Later, as I read my transcripts, I could see how I tried to guide the interview but finally gave up. Babe Montgomery had a story to tell, and it wasn't just about cowgirling or horsemanship.

KMC: I have some questions that I have been asking other women living the valley.

BM: Oh.

KMC: I'm looking at how you answer in a similar or different way from them. Okay?

BM: Well, I don't think like a woman.

KMC: Okay. Well, that's good. Okay.

BM: I guess I think like a bi.

KMC: A bi?

BM: You know . . . a bi?

While I didn't get it at first, it finally dawned on me that she was talking about bisexual women. To Babe though, "bi" meant that despite the fact she was female, she often thought from a masculine point of view.

> I've worked, done men's work all my life, and I have worked with men. I am a great observer. I am not the least bit fond of women mostly because they are influenced by men. It bugs me when I see women (it's about 99 percent of them) who cannot get independent of the male influence. They still have it all sittin' in the back of their heads that they have to be liked by men; and if you are not liked by men, it's just like being an old maid. Now an old bachelor, society is proud of that; but an old maid is derogatory because a woman couldn't catch a man. Who the hell needs one? I mean, it's like we are on the face of the earth for men's benefit. Bullshit! Men don't need it, but they like it. Oh boy, do they like it! I get a lot of reaction from men and women—I'm liked or disliked heartily. (1994)

From the onset of the interview, I knew that Babe Montgomery would tell some good stories. After an hour of talk about her life as an alcoholic, a World War II veteran, a riveter at Boeing during and after the war, a manager of a hotel in Tacoma, Washington, and the winter caretaker at the original Sun Mountain Lodge, she jumped up, announcing, "I'm gonna stop now." Babe took me out to the barn to pull the tack she'd need to get her horses, which were a quarter mile up the road in a neighbor's pasture. In addition to my husband almost backing off a cliff with his horse (see preface), two experiences framed my fear of horses. The first took place when I was a teenager visiting Ocean Shores,

Babe Montgomery pulling tack, 1994. Photograph courtesy of Kristin M. McAndrews

Washington, when my feet flipped out of the stirrups as my horse raced wildly down the beach behind my boyfriend's stallion. In my second incident, a friend brought her horse over to my house. As I petted the horse's flank, the horse looked back at me and bucked, kicking me in the knee. I was wary of horses.

Babe had four horses she needed to take back to her barn but decided to take only two at a time because of my lack of horse sense. She led two of the horses out of the pasture and started down the road. Suddenly, a neighbor revved up his lawn mower, and the horses began to kick. I jumped out of the way. The neighbor stopped the mower and yelled at me. "Hell, what's wrong with you? Why can't you help Babe?"

"I guess I could," I said, probably in a whiny tone.

"I don't know, Walt," Babe called. "She doesn't know much about horses."

Walt, the neighbor, walked closer to the fence. "You afraid of horses?" he barked at me.

"Yes, I guess I am, a little."

The neighbor walked away shaking his head.

The horses towered over me. I must have looked scared as Babe reluctantly gave me one of the lead ropes.

"You watch out for this Arab, he's a biter," she said.

Oh, great. I followed Babe. She kept talking, but I couldn't hear her because of the wind, the horses clopping along the road, and the blood beating in my ears. I tried to keep the lead rope long enough so the horse wouldn't have access to my triceps. My horse kept trotting up to my arm and taking nips at my flesh. I made small shrieks and quietly called the horse an asshole. Of course every time Babe asked how I was doing, the Arab looked innocent and I was too embarrassed about my horse ineptitude to complain. Back at the barn, we tied up the horses and walked together down the road for the next two, my heart racing.

While Babe Montgomery would seem to be an exception to the rule, for many Methow Valley horsewomen their cultural reality is living and working within at least two codes—male and female—and regardless of how they feel about it, they must constantly negotiate between these realms. Nor do they lack models or support in this task. Though they might seem to be oddities in popular culture, the horsewomen I talked to are only a few of the many working cowgirls or horsewomen in the Methow Valley. All the women I interviewed were complete professionals in their fields who would have a great time whooping it up over a tourist caricature emulating Dale Evans, with shiny boots, a perfect hairdo, and meticulously clean clothes, showing up for a trail ride.

And yet, though they get a lot dirtier, like Dale, these horsewomen must metaphorically ride both sides of the horse, with one leg in the wilderness and one at home. At the time I began the interviews, all but three of my subjects were unmarried, but with the exception of Babe Montgomery, all of them had children or stepchildren. While as packers, horse trainers, veterinarians, wranglers, cooks, or trail guides they may occupy a dominant sphere, as women they still inhabit that subordinate sphere that types them as domestics and jokes. Nor is this state of affairs in any way unique. These women necessarily live and work within two worlds—male and female—and, within that, a third realm of tourism. To negotiate this life, horsewomen ground themselves in domestic cultural codes adopted by other women in other places or other times as well. But these horsewomen also enter far enough into the dominant western codes to get their job completed and in the way they want it done. In the world of packing and trail riding, following its conventions to some degree is the only way to succeed professionally. To do this, the women's language must echo the male-inflected cowboy culture—a culture they work within and even market quite successfully to outsiders.

What I have found especially interesting is that the horsewomen's deeply felt knowledge that they are, on some level, interlopers often makes them more successful than conventional cowboys when dealing with outsiders and dangerous situations. These women undeniably use language in ways that reproduce the cowboy culture they inhabit. But when instructing and leading outsiders, who usually don't know much about horses, the horsewomen often seem able to help their guests overcome their own fears even though such encouraging messages must be to some degree covert, because empathy, or even sympathy, for the tourist is unacceptable within that western working code that views both outsiders and women as incompetent intruders into the male preserve of Nature. Joking is often the way these women resolve this opposition. Simply by participating in a typically male-dominated profession, the horsewomen have already to some degree "[opened] up the paternal narrative to what it excludes" (Radner 1993, 6). But to successfully appropriate the language and occupations of cowboy culture, the horsewoman must somehow subvert or rebel against the limitations that such conventions impose even while reproducing them. The women I interviewed took great pride in their success at this task. Their recasting of cowboy language does not seem inconclusive or broken to them—they see no briefly glimpsed openings for bursts of hidden culture, that "buried language" or "fleeting thing" Auerbach identifies as the female literary code. However complex the internal dynamics may be, the stories these women told me generally end with a solid, emphatic resolution—a well-tested secret, offered to the female outsider and interviewer, which reveals how the teller learned to integrate, often through humor, her professional, social, and personal life.

As I conducted my interviews, I found that asking for a scary story that focused on a horse experience generally produced more interesting information about the horsewoman's use of humor for combining codes than my asking for a funny story. Nor should this be especially surprising, since for a horsewoman, "scary" usually combines fear of personal injury with the anxiety of falling short of the standard set by western male-dominant culture. Failing is as frightening as dying, and when it came to fear, I found that horsewomen heartily agreed with other wranglers that a horse wreck stood at the pinnacle of western terror.

Horse-wreck scenes have always been a common motif in western art and literature. Through card art, paintings, and storytelling, horse wrecks haunt the Methow Valley horse community. In the artistic presentations, usually entitled "End of the Line," a cowboy and a horse dangle hopelessly at the end of a rope over a gaping abyss, with the rest of the trail animals about to follow them over the edge to a shared doom.[7] Women do not generally figure in these scenes, unless as comic butts. From 1992 to 2002 I looked in Winthrop shops for depictions of women in "End of the Line" card art. The one female-focused card I found was shockingly insistent on its "comic" nature. The "butt" is a middle-aged woman whose horse clings to the edge of a crumbling cliff with the top of its hooves. The angle is so precarious that the women's elongated breasts hang down over the sides of her arms, pointed toward the abyss below. The image is supposed to be funny, but even if she has a chance of surviving the horse wreck, she certainly has no chance of aging with dignity. This is the fate of middle-aged horsewomen in the American West.

In a community like the Methow Valley, where outfitting tourists is a thriving business and working for the Forest Service is a privilege, horse wrecks remain all-too-possible disasters one tries to avoid but sometimes cannot. Perhaps predictably, then, when asked for their scariest work-related experience, most of my informants described horse wrecks.

After my first pack trip in the Sawtooth Mountain range, I told the outfitter, Claude Miller, about my sickening, sweating fear while riding over Horsehead Pass, elevation 7,500 feet. Claude led me into his living room, where a vividly colored oil painting hanging over an easy chair commemorated his worst horse wreck. There he was, with his team of horses and mules, plunging headlong over a precipice. And yet, although nothing in the painting suggested anything could possibly survive what seemed to be a fall into a bottomless pit, Claude implied that while I should be afraid of something like this happening, with the right outfitter one could survive.

Perhaps he and his painting were pulling this female greenhorn's leg, but I couldn't help wondering how he had gotten out of the situation. Did he have help? Were he and his pack animals hurt? And above all, who cleaned up the mess? Weren't there animal and human bodies to contend with and pack gear scattered to kingdom come? Often the horsewomen's stories answered such questions, providing a cohesive conclusion to the story. Marva Mountjoy, for instance, made sure to tell me that after her horse rolled over on her when the trail gave way during a heavy rain, she rode out fifteen miles with six broken ribs and a serious facial cut. She spent the late fall of 1995 recovering. I found Marva's story both frightening and enlightening. She was as courageous and tough as any cowboy might have been with the same injuries. She didn't whine or complain or ask for a helicopter to take her out of the wilderness. With one other packer, she got herself out of an extremely difficult situation.

Virginia Bennett, a local performer and poet, said, "See, to me, fear, it means, well, if something happens real fast, I'm not fearing right then. But if I got a horse pulling a runaway or something, well right in there I can feel fear. But because things are happening real fast, fear happens later" (1999). Courage and competence come first in dangerous situations. These horsewomen don't freeze or faint away in difficult circumstances; fear arises in retrospect. Lynn Breaky-Clark recalled when her husband abandoned her in a wilderness cabin with their two small children, one an infant. When she began to run out of food for her and her children, she went hunting. On horseback, in deep snow, she managed to kill an elk in order to feed her family. During a September 2002 high hunt in the Pasayten Wilderness, for example, Judy Mally-Burkhart almost completely severed her right thumb as she tied up a fussy horse. It happened in a split second, when she got her thumb stuck between a lead rope and a piece of metal on the wood post she was tying the horse to. The horse pulled his head back, and "off came the thumb down to two slivers—a nerve and a vein" (2003). Alone at camp with some forty-five horses and mules, Judy closed her fingers around the thumb, wrote a message in blood for her husband on a paper plate, and drove down Hart's Pass, one of the most dangerous roads in Washington State. She kept her fingers closed over the thumb even as she had to shift the gears in the large old truck she drove. "My dog Barney always rides up front with me, but I made him ride in the back so if I dropped my thumb he couldn't eat it," she recalled. She stopped a Forest Service truck, which had a radio, explained the situation, and asked that an ambulance be called to Mazama. Judy spent twenty days at Harborview Hospital in Seattle after her thumb was reattached. "It was touch and go for a couple of months whether or not I was going to lose that thumb," she said. "It's only been a couple of months since I've been able to even talk about it or even laugh at how ridiculous it was, especially driving down that road one handed and trying to shift. I was praying" (2003). As in many of these women's stories, fear is displaced by humor in performance. Like any good western hero, these women get right back on the horse. They all too frequently have to exhibit courage in the face of some pretty difficult circumstances.

When I interviewed Virginia Bennett, she and her husband were working as ranch managers of Tice Ranch in Twisp, Washington. The owner of the ranch often invited Virginia to recite poetry or sing for his guests. While she was a newcomer to the Methow Valley, Virginia was well known and respected for her hard work, writing, and musical talent. A practiced storyteller, she shared well-constructed and funny stories. Or as she put it, "All the stories I tell kind of turn funny. I guess because of the way I tell them." For horse-wreck tales, Virginia told the following:

When Your Boot Is Right Hangin'

I had a mule I was breakin' in Colorado. I had just came out of the arena on him. I was goin' to ride him back to the barn. Suddenly, he bolted. A mule will run away more than he'll buck. Although, I've been bucked off before.

He bolted, with me, towards a big drop-off. In Aspen, Colorado, it's very steep country. He ran right straight for a big cliff. I pulled his head around to turn him from running there. With a mule you can pull their head all the way back to your lap and they can still run right straight. And, he was still runnin' straight.

So finally, I was in a position so I could jump off. I let his head go and he looked around in front of him. Mules are real smart. He saw where he was heading and got right to the edge, and he stopped. Like he was thinking, "If you would have let me see this before, I would have stopped a long time ago."

And that's like when your boot is right hangin' out over the edge of the thing, and you go, "Whoa! That was close!" (1999)

Virginia is not the typical cowboy horse trainer—she employs gentler techniques to civilizing horses and mules. Despite her assurance that she trains
her animals using patience and persistence, by her starting off the story with
"breakin'" the audience automatically receives an image of violence. I wasn't
sure what she was doing in the arena, but she was probably making the mule
ride circles, perhaps to bore him into submission. When the mule bolts, it is
a surprise to Virginia and to the listener—although we both understand the
unpredictability of mules. The image of the mule's body running straight for
a steep cliff with its head pulled back upon Virginia's lap is comic—an "End
of the Line" sort of humor. But in this anecdote, the mule finally sees his possible plunge over the cliff once Virginia lets go of the reins, and it stops right
at the edge of the abyss. When she recalls that the mule "was thinking, 'If you
would have let me see this before, I would have stopped a long time ago,'" it
suggests that Virginia was the one responsible for the possible wreck, not the
mule. It was a close call with her riding boot "right hanging over the edge of
the thing." Self-deprecation and understatement are hallmarks of both cowboy culture and women's humor.

In the next story Virginia is not as lucky at avoiding a wreck, nor does her
horse have the same self-consciousness as the mule in the story above.

Breakin' Virginia

There was a little gal up the road [in New Mexico], and her mother had asked
me to coach her on barrel racing. So I rode this big quarter horse—about seven
years old, but he wasn't a colt. [The girl's father had bought the horse for barrel
racing, but the horse been raced.] All he knew was to race. In New Mexico, on
the reservations, they have all these match races, which they bet on and stuff.
This horse had been match raced. This horse had been raced so much that it
was a nervous wreck—a complete nervous wreck. So I was trying to gentle him
and calm him down and stuff. His name was Fooler. I rode him up the road to
the girl's house. I tied him to a tree.

It was hot. The mom came out and asked me if I wanted a beer.

"No," I said.

So I was watching the girl and giving her a few pointers about running the
barrels. Finally, it was time to get home. So I went and untied Fooler. He'd just

been standing there. There was no reason for him to be nervous. Probably, in retrospect, there were other horses running around, but even they weren't running very close to him. I said bye to everyone.

I barely set in the saddle when he reared up and went over backwards on me. And he was ON me! Then, he got up and ran off.

The mother came over. My glasses were gone. I had dirt up my nose and a hurt leg.

"Do you want a beer now?" she says.

"Yeah," I said. (1999)

After she told this story, I asked Virginia about her injuries. She had a pretty swollen leg, but after she drank the cold beer, she had to get back to the business of finding Fooler and riding him back home. Like many of the horse-wreck stories I heard, "Breakin' Virginia" maintains the idea that the horse or mule is out of control, and not necessarily because of anything that the horsewoman has done to provoke the incident. In this case Fooler had been raced, too young, on the reservation. Perhaps he was made nervous by the other horses at the ranch where Virginia was tutoring the girl in barrel racing. Barrel racing is a fast-paced rodeo event, specifically created for women. In both of Virginia's horse-wreck tales, the consequences are humorous but rather small.

In Lauralee Northcott's scary story "They're Just Devils," she has a horse wreck aggravated by a swarm of bees, plus the packers she's working for tease and play a practical joke on her, generally making the experience even more harrowing. In this story she was on a pack trip for the Forest Service in the Pasayten Wilderness. The packer started to tell her a scary story about the narrow and steep trail they were riding on near the headwaters of the Methow River. Swaying back and forth, the packer leaned into the hill and out over the sheer cliff above the river, demonstrating what not to do. Suddenly, another packer's string of horses and mules was coming down the trail, which was a narrow ledge. Since there was no way to get off to the side of the trail, the horses and mules began to have a wreck. One mule ended up covered by another mule. Lauralee stayed on her horse, while the packer dismounted to try and straighten out the stock.

THEY'RE JUST DEVILS

So I had to hold the packer's horse, his string [of mules and horses], and my horses. I was backed up to this other mule train. And these guys were trying to fix the situation. So this horse I'm on—Judy—is sniffing. And she starts pawin' the ground. Well, she paws up a goddamn bees' nest. These are ground bees that time of year in the fall. And there were bees all over me.

So I got bees all over me, and they're stinging the horses, and Judy's rearing because she's getting stung. And there's no place to go, 'cause we're in a bad place. So I decide it's either me or the pack string, and I'm gonna save me. So I let go of Brandon's stuff. It's history. And all I'm doin' is staying on Judy.

So finally, she gets herself away from 'em enough and she's a good girl, 'cause she doesn't do any more than that. And that's it. So time to settle down.

So I looked back and there's Brandon and Eric and they're both just lookin' right at me. And I know that they're scared—at least at first. But then—they're just devils, those packers. They're just devils, you know. They're just lookin' at me.

"Uh, Lauralee," said Brandon.

"Yeah."

"If you could get my horse's reins and just walk around that one tree, that whole pack string's gonna straighten out," he said. "Would you do that? 'Cause they're in a jumble."

I looked at him. I thought, if I don't have to get off my horse, maybe I'll do that. So I leaned over and I got ahold of the reins and I walked around that tree. And sure enough, he was right. They all just straightened right out. And when I looked back—I was real proud of myself.

I turned to the packers and they were gone. They'd gone down to the river to get water. And they made me just sit there for ten minutes.

I was just boilin' mad. I got up on top of my stirrups to look at 'em and they were down by the river, just laughin' their guts out. (2005).

Because she is a performer and a teacher, Lauralee has a talent for storytelling. In the telling, "They're Just Devils" is funny and well constructed.

In the summer of 2000, I interviewed and photographed Betsy Devin-Smith in her home on the Methow River. I had heard about Betsy from a

Lauralee Northcott pulling fence, 2004.
Photograph courtesy of Lauralee Northcott

number of other women, and I was encouraged by her brother, Steve Devin, to interview her. When I asked about how horses figured into her veterinary practice, she responded, "I think I have a pretty good way with horses. It's kind of a nonverbal communication and feel for them. That's because I work with them all the time, every day. So, I think I'm pretty good at being with them. But I'm not just a horse vet. I do all animals" (2000). An avid horsewoman, she told me that "moving cows" is her horse specialty. She spoke about moving cattle on Stud Horse Mountain, which is now covered with homes. During our interview she seemed nostalgic for the past, when the Methow Valley was less developed, but "the community is growing so fast. I have seen much change since I was a kid." A vibrant, enthusiastic storyteller, Betsy invited me into the home she and her husband Skip built. After our interview she gave me a tour of her small ranch, where she raises sheep and chickens. At the time, she also ran a herd of cattle in the Pasayten National Forest.

Like many of the women I spoke to, Betsy said that as a child she had a strong desire to ride and work in the wilderness.[8] Also like many women in the valley, she had worked for North Cascades Safari and Claude Miller.

I worked for him for about ten years. I started out as a flunky—water carrier, cook's helper, and dishwasher. I worked under Ann [Henry]. I cooked for awhile too.

I did a little bit of packing, but women don't pack. Actually when I was a kid, all I wanted to do was to be a packer. I'd go into the backcountry and watch the guys. I'd watch and watch and watch. And every so often someone would say, we'd better manny that up. I'd go, Oh yeah! I could tie it [the manny] because I'd watched them so many times. So one time Claude was shorthanded with packers. Here I am! I can do it! So he let me take the guests in. And everybody was

Betsy Devin-Smith herding sheep, 2005. Photograph courtesy of Leslie Lanthorn

fine. Claude said, "by golly, I guess women can pack, but I don't know, though."
I went back to cooking. (2000)

As a young woman, Betsy also worked for the Forest Service. She and another packer were on their way out of Hidden Lakes, coming down Eight-Mile Pass after having delivered supplies to a Forest Service trail crew.[9] Betsy's partner was leading a string of five mules, and she followed with a string of four mules and a horse.

Pinned Down

Horses aren't, it seems like, as smart as mules. If you have a tree, all the mules will figure out which side of the tree to go around, but here comes a horse, who goes around the wrong side. The horse ends up pulling back and breaking a rope—like that. Well, I don't know exactly what happened, but this horse on my string must have gotten stung by a bee or something because he just came up on me. And the way he came up on me, it happened so fast. The rope that I was leading him with came around on the other side of my horse. This horse knocked my horse down. I was pinned down. And this loose horse came and fell on top of us too!

It happened so fast. I was under my horse thinking, this isn't a good situation because of what was tied to this other horse—four or five mules. I knew the place on the trail where we were piled up was pretty steep on the side. I thought I better get out of this. It wasn't comfortable.

I always carry a pocketknife with me, but the way my hands were under the horse, and with the ropes and the animals on me, I couldn't get to my knife quick enough. The horses weren't just sitting there contented. Things were heating up. Everything was tense. I thought, I'm gonna die right here on this trail. Suddenly it was just a flurry of critters and mules, because now the whole string was starting to come over us and thrashing and rolling. It was just by the grace of God somehow I ended up rolling off the trail, being pushed or kicked or moved off the trail and down the cliff—which was great! Really!

Maybe this should have been a funny story.

Luckily there was a log on the cliff that stopped me. All my critters blew up, with packs flying, and mules and horses and everything headed down the trail. The guy that I was with, he was in front of me. So when all the dust kind of stopped, I hauled myself back up to the trail thinking, I can't believe I'm still alive. I was!

And where was my buddy? He thought I was dead. He also thought the mules were more important than me. He went to get them. Later he said that when he looked back and saw the mules were kicking me right in the head, or at least he thought they were, he said there was no way I could have been alive. So he stopped all the mules and the rest of them from heading everywhere.

I was pretty tender. I could crawl for awhile. Then I thought, I better walk, but I couldn't walk very far. So I thought the best thing would be to ride, because maybe I could ride out. That was better. Luckily, I wasn't too far from the trailhead. I thought I had done something to my kidneys or something, but I was just sore for three or four days.

That incident was scary. (2000)

Betsy's narrative commences with a typical disclaimer as to the cause of the wreck. It was not directly the fault of the wrangler or horsewoman; the famously unpredictable horses or mules (see following story) were responsible for the death-defying results. The audience suspends its disbelief as Betsy recalls her thoughts during the four- to five-minute harrowing experience. Animated in the telling, she gestures, modulates her voice, and makes facial expressions. And even though the story begins with a serious tone, as she visualizes how the wreck must have looked to an outsider, she realizes how humorous it might seem. After describing the scene of the string pig pile, she actually started laughing at the incongruous image of a small young woman squished beneath a pile of squirming, flailing horse stock. And the image is kind of funny as long as the narrator's laughing herself. It is especially funny in light of the fact that she uses words to subordinate the rush and violence of the string racing toward her fallen horse. When she says that the horses "came" or "came up" on her, it might provoke images that the horse and mules were gently ambling along the trail. But in fact, they were pounding, kicking, blasting, and bearing down on Betsy's horse—and on Betsy, still pinned beneath. Using language that sublimates or trivializes the import of the experience is another way that Betsy's narrative reflects a cowboy Code of the West. Despite the possibility of injury and maybe death, Betsy finds a way out of the mess. And even though the other packer has left her for dead and gone to collect the runaway stock, she understands that things like this happen in the wilderness. She exhibits courage, strength, and a willingness to get right back on the horse. She survived a "good" horse wreck and lived to tell the tale of it in a quiet but humorous manner.

Meghan Sullivan related one of her scariest stories, which focused on her mother, Shiril Cairns.

What Was She Thinkin'?

The stories that I think of are the ones I heard my mother tell. Not personally that have happened to me—except the scary one. I was thinking about funny. I can't think of my own funny story that wasn't something my mom told. I think that's really interesting. But so scary was actually involving my mom.

We had rounded up these wild mustangs. I wasn't on the roundup—I was with the kids. But Dave [Meghan's husband] and Mom and Jessie and Joseph and all these people went down and rounded up these wild mustangs which were running on the hills above Pateros.

That's where those two gray fillies that I'm working now came from. They were wild mustangs.

Since Dave and I were going to start operating the ranch more, Mom was going to stay at her red house and work these wild horses. That's what she really wanted to do. There were two three-year-old stallions, a two-year-old stallion, and the year-old filly that I have now. And so they spent all day.

Mom had a heat stroke. She had a seizure out there in the middle of the woods while catching these horses. It was a long hard day of driving horses. It's hard to drive a horse because they are so fast. They don't get tired and there's all this open space. But they got the horses to the corral and put them in the stock truck. They just chased the two older stallions in. Then they took them up to the red house. Mom was in the stock truck with these two wild horses trying to get halters on them. She knew if she turned them out into her pasture, she was never going to get a halter on them. So she had these long lead lines just to let them drag these lead lines so she could work with them. But these horses had never seen a person. Never been touched by a person. They were totally wild two-year-olds. And they were big horses.

So she's in the stock truck—which is scary enough. You hear all this CRASH! CRASH! BANG! BANG! I am standing there with the kids—all these people were there. Mom decided to ride one of her sound riding horses and dally the lead rope of one of the stallions around the saddle horn. She had to get like seven hundred yards from where the stock truck was to where she wanted these horses in the corral. You couldn't unload the horses over there because there was no unloading ramp.

So that was her theory. According to her, she is just going to drag this horse over to the corral. She gets the rope good and short and she comes out of the stock truck. But as soon as that horse sees that open space, he just goes ballistic. She jumps off the riding horse. I don't know what she was thinkin'!

She was the most stubborn . . . she'd get something into her head and she wasn't going to change it.

So she's holding onto the lead rope of this wild horse and trying to get him in the direction of the corral. But he's rearing. He's bucking. He's kicking. He's all over the place. The rope is tangled up in everything. And then she gets tangled up in the rope. And the horse is dragging her. She's trying to pull herself up; hand over hand, higher up to his head so she can get better control.

Or what? I don't know. And we're all seeing this. And it's my mom, who is like 115 pounds, against this thousand-pound wild horse that had never been touched by a person before.

She ends up getting high enough up on his head, but something happens with the rope. Now he's running over the top of her, repeatedly. He's dragging her along and she's just underneath him. He's just pounding her.

She just laid there. She let go of the rope—FINALLY. She just laid there. And I thought, oh my god, she's dead. It was just horrible. There was nothing you could do watching this horrible thing. I ran over to her.

She was laying on the ground—all beat up.

"Well, that was a really stupid idea, wasn't it?" she said. (2000)

Meghan's storytelling was animated. During the telling, she was clearly upset about this memory. But typical of Shiril, she makes light of the entire wreck in a self-mocking manner. Some critics have explained self-deprecation as typical of women's humor.

Kit McLean Cramer's scary anecdote displays most fully how horsewomen can simultaneously invoke the horse wreck's narrative power and recast this heroic tradition by humorously introducing feminist or tourist themes.

My Worst, Most Spectacular Wreck

You know, nothing has ever happened to me that I thought was life and death—had a situation that scared me bad. I remember one that gave me the shakes the worst, just 'cause it took forever. God, it was this awful wreck. Claude and them took a huge camp out the day before, during high hunt, from Sheep Mountain, and they'd taken all the good mules with them. Well, I go out the next morning to run in the mules to take out to Court's Lake. And I was by myself. And there's one good mule, that's just Whistler up there at Sun Mountain, and six of the snortiest wild little ornery sons of bitches you've ever seen in your life.

It was the Harder mules.[10] They're little round-back wild little things. They're all dragging lead ropes 'cause you can't catch them. Anyway, I just kind of went—Oh. My. God. But that's life.

Anyway, I got those hunter guys on their horses and sent them out, you know. We do that during high hunt. There you go. So I got them out of there and I started packing up these mules. So I got them all caught up and tied together and headed over to Courts Lake and got there.

So there I am. These guys had made their own pack boxes. They'd painted them and they were very slippery. Because it was the end of the trip, all their boxes hardly weighed anything. They were very light. There was nothing in them, much. They had a couple of plastic ice chests that were empty. So I'm sneaking around packing up these whoopee-snortie-little mules and get everything on there. I got everything lined out and tied on. I looked at the packing job and thought, that's a *big no no*—a rope was dangling. These mules were so wild. I didn't want no accidents. So I took a rope that was dangling just a little bit too far and I lifted it up around the plastic handle of one of the plastic ice chests. I tied one little small, you know, shoelace just to cross and put under and pulled it tight on the handle 'cause of that dangly little rope. I didn't want it down there where it'd, you know, start causing any wrecks. I looked at it at the time and thought that's kind of dumb but did it anyway.

I went probably five miles down the trail. I went out over Sand Ridge and out through Whistler Basin and up over the top of the notch there. Going around that top's very steep and you're out in the middle of ten thousand acres of meadow—without a tree for miles! Actually, it was probably about a mile to the bottom where there was some timber, which was no good to me.

Anyway, that plastic ice chest that didn't weigh anything kind of popped out of the sling. Which usually wouldn't of been a FALL-OUT-BIG SPOOK, but usually you get everything stopped. Well, I had the top of one of those plastic ice chests tied on by that one little string. Well, the wreck was on.

Usually, when you get into a deal like that, you hang them [mules] up in the trees. You know, or circle them around and everything kind of comes to a stop. But I was up there by myself and every one of them just blew up. Those wild little mules, every one of them's bucking. They got all wound up in that little thing and turned around and started to run back the other way. I'm on this hillside that's just steeper than a cow's face, and finally, turn around and just bolted all the way to the top. I thought I'd just kind of wear them out a little bit. I was on a good mountain horse, which was kind of unusual 'cause I ride a lot of colts. But I was riding old Smoky. We went up to the top. I finally got them all wound up and stopped.

But Whistler, the one good mule that I was leading, had a deer on him.[11] When I got everything stopped, I had the deer horns jabbing on my ribs. Whistler was pissed. He had no sense of humor about all that kind of monkeyshines. He is a good pack mule, but he was so mad. The look on his face—well, if I wouldn't've been so scared, I'd've laughed. And those deer horns were still jabbed into my ribs. I had a rope burn about this long across my back [gestures about twelve inches] I took a long time to heal, because rope burns take a long time to heal. And, one foot was hung up on the rope and kind of pulled over to the horse's rump. So, I was a bit tangled up but that wasn't particularly dangerous. I finally got everything stopped.

All those little mules had unloaded that gear all over. All those slick boxes just popped out of those slings right and left. I had shit scattered from heck to breakfast. Here, I'm up there by myself. I managed to find one little scrawny low juniper bush that had Smoky tied to it and had Whistler tied to him. I finally got all these little mules kind of lined up behind 'em.

You know, when this whole thing started there was a camp down at the bottom of the hill. They'd seen this whole thing start, and started hiking up to rescue me or something. Or to get closer, so they could watch. I'm not sure. But when this was all said and done, I stepped off that horse and my knees just collapsed. I had the shakes so bad just from those post-adrenaline shakes. I'd do that at the racetrack, too.[12] When I'd catch a really bad runaway, I'd shake—it was my adrenaline. I tried to stand up and whomp, slap, down I went—hit the ground.

Anyway, I put them back together and headed out. But that's probably the worst, most spectacular wreck I've ever had in my life. I just couldn't stop it. God. It probably went on for twenty minutes, but I'm sure it was only four or five minutes. It's hard to tell when you get in those things. But it absolutely almost gave me a heart attack. Because I couldn't stop them. And I thought, if I let go of them I'll never see them again. And I couldn't have let go of this whole thing, or I'd've lost them, you know? They'd've took off. It was wild!

I was walking around the hill gathering up stuff. I don't know what those people [the hunters she was packing for] thought of all the grass. I was so upset, I was running around this hillside scraping their stuff back in the boxes, grabbing all their gear that was scattered because the lids come off the boxes and there's toothbrushes and underwear and everything else laying all over the hillside. So I'm grabbing it with clumps of old grasses and throw it back in the boxes. I have no idea what they thought.

But that was probably my worst wreck. (1995)

Kit's story shows the shaping influences of both cowboy and contemporary culture. Just the choice of subject would place her story within the traditions of the American West. As the ultimate nightmare for working packers, the horse wreck not only commands cowboy interest, but also supplies a standard for measuring the victim-hero's expertise. Strong and self-reliant though isolated from her peers, Kit manages to save the animals and herself. In the process she passes successfully the harshest of all trail initiation rites and lays claim to the status of western hero. And yet another western tradition also informs this narrative—a resistance to women's entering a male domain, which Kit suggests might have been at least partially responsible for causing the wreck. Though not explicitly barred from her chosen profession, she is left with inferior stock, "the Harder mules," because her boss and perhaps another couple of wranglers have already taken off with most of the gear—and the best horses and mules.

Here the roles of woman and trail rookie coalesce in Kit. Perhaps in part because it teaches them to be flexible and creative in dangerous circumstances, traditionally pack wranglers, the least experienced members of the trail crew, get the most difficult stock to work with. But in this case the terrain and the guests combine to place Kit in a dangerous, potentially life-threatening situation, and she implicitly criticizes her boss for making this possible. The scene itself, "out in the middle of ten thousand acres of meadow—without a tree for miles," may not at first seem especially dangerous, but the slope is "steeper than a cow's face" and the lack of trees means there is almost nothing in the environment that Kit can use to stop the wreck once it gets started. A single bush becomes her anchor for Smoky, Whistler, and all the Harder mules—a very fragile tool for warding off disaster. The tourists themselves pose a double problem. First, they are not present when things start happening, and even though they probably wouldn't have been much help, their absence contributes to Kit's isolation. More seriously though, tourist ignorance not only actually sets off the wreck, but also compounds Kit's problems once it gets started. Those nicely painted boxes and ice chests the tourists have brought along are more appropriate for a picnic or car camping than a pack trip. Pack boxes are made of plywood and covered with Varathane—the opposite of slick—and everything not in a box is wrapped in a manny (a large square of canvas) then tied in huge bundles onto the sides of the mules. The results of tourist innocence here are all too predictable. When an ice chest slips out of its sling, it startles the mules and begins the wreck, which gets progressively worse as those slick pack boxes fly off the sides of the bucking animals.

As a woman, Kit must not only deal with the wreck itself, but also feel the additional pressure of taking into account how her performance looks—to the actual witnesses, hiking up from the camp below to "rescue" or "watch" her; to her boss; to the hunter guests; to the larger Winthrop community; and eventually, even to me. An unstated male presence pervades the event, and I would argue that one of Kit's narrative goals in "My Worst, Most Spectacular Wreck" is to show how her experience was actually challenging and her own performance heroic. The degree of difficulty is the issue. Take, for example, the setting. Although certainly terrifying, the traditional gaping-abyss horse wreck (as depicted in Claude Miller's painting and "End of the Line" card art) is uncomplicated. The chaos will presumably end when the hero and his trail animals hit bottom. In contrast, because the steep meadow stretches for acres and acres, Kit must somehow bring the wreck to an end personally—a fact she emphasizes by saying that while it felt like twenty minutes, the chaos only lasted about four or five, which is still an eternity when compared to the quick plunge over a cliff. The same kind of contrast operates between the traditional notions of the wreck and Kit's account of her actions. Usually, many possible questions about the hero go unasked. What was the reason for the dangerous trip in the first place? Was it a good idea to be leading so many animals next to a cliff alone? Why did the animals go out of control, and could the hero have prevented it? Through a mixture of humor and confession, Kit answers these questions, and in the process she implicitly suggests that such questions might be interesting ones to pose to other, more traditional horse-wreck survivors.

Kit's honesty is disarming, but also thought provoking, and perhaps subversive as well. Take, for example, her admission that the way she secured one of the ice chests was "kind of dumb." As Radner (1993) has noted, such claims of incompetence can be a female coding strategy; in Kit's case they draw attention to the fact that at least she anticipated trouble and tried, however unsuccessfully, to *prevent* the wreck. Similarly, Kit reveals that once it was on, her major concern was to keep the wreck from escalating into a "FALL-OUT-BIG SPOOK," clearly a term for the kind of total disaster celebrated in typical horse-wreck tales. This source of Kit's fear also separates her from the wreck tradition. The big achievement is having survived a "FALL-OUT-BIG SPOOK"; whatever fear, if any, will arise from impending death. Kit, however, repeatedly says that she was terrified—"it almost gave me a heart attack"—by the possibility that she would completely lose control.

For the fact of the matter is that unlike her traditional horse-wreck counterparts, Kit not only succeeds in preventing total disaster but manages to do so in a manner that meets her professional responsibilities as a horsewoman in the tourist business and, ironically enough, her assumed duties as a "traditional" woman as well. Like a male hero, by bringing her story back to the community and telling it to her boss, her peers, and eventually, me, Kit claims her place in the horse-wreck survivors' club. The story she actually tells, however, at the very least calls into question this club's traditions. She stresses, for example, that except for the pack animals, she's alone in the wilderness, with no one to help her or answer her questions. Even though Kit succeeds in preventing a total wreck, she still makes it clear that she felt tricked or forced into this solitary triumph. Nor does she leave her story in the realm of high terror or adventure. She has just barely saved herself, her employer's animals, and the tourists' possessions, and still Kit immediately remembers her professional duties. She is still on a deadline. Her boss, the other wranglers, and the hunters will be waiting for her at the end of the trail with the stock and gear trucks, so regardless of how she might feel about all of these men at the moment, she collects the "stuff" scattered "from heck to breakfast" on the hill.

At one level Kit's frantic, unorganized attempt to jam the hunters' belongings, along with a fair amount of grass, back into whatever worthless pack box comes to hand seems to fit into the tradition of mocking the greenhorn. As a professional horsewoman, she cannot explicitly let the tourists know that at one point she lost control. But in doing her duty, she unavoidably prepares a surprise for them, one that will be all the more puzzling because Kit never explains it. Only the western community gets let in on the secret and therefore gets to laugh at the idea of the hunters' opening up their boxes at home. On another level, however, the outlines of the story are all too familiar. Once again, though it's actually the product of male stupidity and thoughtlessness, a woman finds herself cleaning up the mess. It is at this point that Kit's story may be sharing a coded message with one segment of her audience—a message that, while available to the public at large, is basically incomprehensible to the male-dominant community. Radner notes that some linguists have identified such "feminist messages," which are "critical of some aspects of women's subordination," as "characteristic of 'women's language' or 'language of the powerless'" (1993, 3). I certainly found myself understanding and empathizing with Kit's obligation to clean up after men, and other moments in her story seemed oriented toward a female audience as well.

Most obviously, Kit's admission of fear to the point of collapse, not only during the event but afterward as well, would probably never find its way into

Kit McLean Cramer on a sleigh ride at Sun Mountain, 2002.
Photograph courtesy of Kit McLean Cramer

a cowboy horse-wreck narrative. Though a cowboy might admit to almost getting a heart attack in the middle of things, and he would probably be happy to exhibit the scar from a twelve- to eighteen-inch rope burn, it's hard to imagine him describing "those post-adrenaline shakes" that cause Kit to fall flat on the ground—shakes she significantly remembers also having after successfully completing other extremely dangerous horse-related tasks such as those at the racetrack. But my strong impression when hearing this story was that Kit had a remarkably funny, self-depreciating manner of telling it. Though it was obviously a serious tale, as Kit told it to me her voice, face, and body were all very expressive. And above all, she laughed, seeming to enjoy making light of the situation. Such laughter distances Kit and her audience from the actual danger and demands of the event, and while downplaying them in a self-deprecating way is often typical of what is considered "women's talk," laughter can also be masking a narrative's subversive power. In this story Kit displays professional skills that make her a success within a male-dominated domain. It is her female point of reference, however, that allows her to surpass even the icons of cowboy culture. Horsemen survive big wrecks. Horsewomen try to prevent them, when possible keep them little ones, and bring themselves, the animals, and all the goods back home unharmed.

And in telling the story to me, Kit acknowledges a shared female perspective. This does not mean she sees me as an equal. Though I know something about the community, her boss, and her work, I'm still a cowgirl wanna-be and an academic tourist. Her story only reaffirms that she is the wilderness expert and I am the dude. I find myself, as the outsider, the scholar, the absentee landowner, and even the woman, getting nudged slightly off balance. And whether intentionally or not, I am positive now that off center is where Kit wanted to put me, still a victim within that cowboy tradition of greening the greenhorn. But then, with less justice, this is the position women like Kit still find themselves occupying. Though horsewomen are prevalent in this and other rural American communities and face the same physical and professional challenges as men, when cowboys and popular culture look for them, they still see Dale Evans—a sidekick but not quite, riding not outside but barely alongside, in the culture's visual, intellectual, and emotional periphery. And as Kit reveals so compellingly, at times you can only laugh.

CHAPTER THREE

TOOLS OF THE TRADE

Humor and Horse Sense

In many rural communities of Washington State, cowgirls or horsewomen have for generations functioned independently and successfully in the wilderness *and* in the domestic realm. These women can pack a mule, survive a horse wreck, cook up a campfire stew on tidbits, raise children, make a living, and tell stories about all of these experiences. Nor can the lives of these women be shoehorned into the stereotypic and restricting profile of the helpful wife.[1] By working with horses and entering rough country, these women cross gender lines within a male-inflected geographic and cultural domain without abandoning the domestic. The horsewomen I interviewed claim the wilderness and professional authority with just as much certainty as men. Assuming the role of knowing figure in a humorous narrative is only one of the many ways in which these horsewomen appropriate male cultural codes. As they recalled humorous, work-related events, these women uncloaked the ways they have coped creatively and intelligently with potentially violent experiences in wilderness settings. In the telling they empower themselves, becoming heroic in their own stories at least partially because they demonstrate their possession of supposedly male power through an easy manipulation of male wilderness props. The humorous narratives and anecdotes of the Methow Valley horsewomen display patterns of authority that would place them solidly within many of the literary traditions of the American West, if such stories could be fully acknowledged.

In this chapter I discuss stories told by Marva Mountjoy, Judy Mally-Burkhart, and Kit McLean Cramer. Marva was described as a good storyteller, a competent horsewoman, and a "real lady." My first interview with Marva took place in 1994 after she had been the head packer on a pack trip I took into the Sawtooth Wilderness. She told me stories in her kitchen while making Basque bread in a Dutch oven for a pack trip the next morning. I interviewed her two more times—once at her home in 1996 and another time with her Bitch and Stitch Club, consisting of a trio of horsewomen who meet once a month for a sleepover to do artwork, quilt, cook, and tell stories.

In the summer of 1996 I rode with Marva and her packer, Rod, again but this time into the Pasayten Wilderness in the North Cascades. I brought the transcribed stories with me so I could share them with Marva. I wanted her thoughts about the following story to see if I had been accurate in my transcription. One day I sat down at Cornwall Lake, about eight miles from our base camp (Spanish Camp), and read my completed transcripts of her stories out loud.

"God," she said, "they sound kind of boring, don't they?"

I assured her that the original performance had been very entertaining. "Something was lost in the transcription," I said, which seemed to reassure her that the relative dullness of the text was my problem, not hers. Nor can this flatness be avoided. Though the horsewomen I interviewed are dynamic, enthusiastic storytellers, the performative dimension of their stories cannot be fully conveyed on paper. Nevertheless, some indication of their dramatic talent for telling tales, which serves so well in these women's tourist-related jobs, or at the very least some indication of the circumstances surrounding the telling needs to be given.

At home Marva looked very different than she did on the trail, with full makeup, her hair done, and a fancy western shirt. She was animated and dramatic in her storytelling. I was delighted with such an engaging performer. It was interesting to me that the written text erased the dynamics of her storytelling, especially some of the humorous dimensions. The audience had shifted from real to abstract. While vivid when they were told, in abstraction Marva's stories were bland for a reading audience.

A talented and experienced performer, Lauralee Northcott's stories also revealed the same flatness when they were transcribed. A freelance cook/packer, she is often hired by outfitters not only for her cooking but for her storytelling ability. And yet two major anecdotes, which were charged with fear and humor in the telling, seemed dreary and confusing in print. The humor evoked for the listening audience was clear, but the context for the humor must be explained for a reading audience.

While the issue of audience must always be addressed when evaluating humorous discourse, it is a formidable concept to unravel. Sigmund Freud's notion of audience, as it pertains to humor, is famously one-dimensional. Not only do all participants in the joke laugh at the same thing, but only two, "the self and the person who is the object," are even needed; "a third person may come into it but it is not essential" (1960, 144). To Freud the laughter produced by a joke is psychical energy, transferred from one person to another. The third person, when there is one, is a collaborator. Of course in Freud's world, joking relationships excluded women. Women could sometimes express wit and mildly appreciate the humor of a joke as an audience, but they could not tell jokes. Zita Dresner points to other factors that perpetuate the assumption that women do not have the capacity for creating humor. Her argument also serves to explain why a reading audience might not be able to appreciate women's humorous discourse:

> Other barriers to the recognition and acceptance of women humorists have been the masculine control of the media and the concomitant condition of both sexes to laugh at what men have defined as humorous, the socialization as women to be submissive rather than aggressive, the contradictions between male and female perception of incongruity, resulting from their different cultural experiences, and the cultivation by women of a humorous style that, both by choice and necessity, has been considered less political, less iconoclastic, less dynamic, and therefore, less significant than the male variety. (1988, 142)

The case of audience becomes more complex in Mikhail Bakhtin's work, which views any utterance as socially diverse phenomenon. He gestures towards heteroglossia, where a multitude of cultural factors must be considered when attempting to identify all the possible dimensions of the tale. Typically in my interviews, in which both informant and field-worker were female, a we/they distinction commonly operating in women's humor appeared. The we/they dialectic is often discussed in critiques of humor. Nancy Walker, for instance, states that

> To laugh at "what you haven't got when you ought to have it" implies a con-
> sciousness of both one's rights and the denial of those rights; to laugh when
> "you wish in your secret heart [that the situation] were not funny" suggests an
> awareness of the disparity and incongruity that members of minority groups
> constantly endure: the distance between the official promise of equality and the
> actual experience of subordination to the dominant culture. (1988, 101–2)

In all cases, though, evaluating the audience is essential in order to determine just who is laughing at whom. Actually, Freud's schematic for humorous discourse works very well for women. As the Methow Valley horsewomen tell their humorous stories, I function as the butt of the joke and as audience. The humorous anecdotes create different positions and attitudes for potential audiences through their multifaceted employment of humor and play. My major concern here is how play becomes both a defense against and an alternative to antagonism and attack.

Gregory Bateson has argued that play and aggression imitate each other so closely that only our ability to "read" the physiological signals of another allows us to distinguish them (1972, 14), and certainly, threats of potential violence pervade some of the horsewomen's narratives.[2] Through the skillful handling of their audience, however, dangerous situations become humorous tales—at least in the telling. Marva's first story, which I've entitled "Pissing Off the Cook," could be taken rather seriously, but since Marva tells it specifically as a humorous tale, the listener must consider where and how the humor intervenes to dispel the potential conflict in the narrative. Two jokes structure the story. The first one is unsuccessful, somewhat murky, and hardly funny, while the second one is recognized and enjoyed by all the participants.

Pissing Off the Cook

We had a man who had been pulling these little pranks on me. He was always putting rocks in my shoes, or something. On the last morning of camp, I ran down to the outhouse. I looked for the toilet paper but couldn't find it. I thought, well, I just coffee-canned it, so it must have blown off the hill or something.[3] But I thought, we're leaving, so it's no big deal anyway.

So, Anita and I were fixing breakfast, and you know how those fires are in the tents, and if you burn the bacon it gets smoky . . . so anyway, it was getting kind of smoky in the tent. I went around back and flipped open the back window and pretty soon we got the front ends all tied up. 'Nita and I are just frying and cooking breakfast like crazy. Finally, one of the guests comes in.

He sits us both down on the kitchen boxes then sits between us and puts his head between his knees for a moment, cause of the smoke. He says, "I've got to hand it to you ladies, you're cool as cucumbers."

And, we're looking at him like, "What are you talking about?" .

He says, "Well, you know that can that was down at the outhouse?"

I said, "Well, hey, it must have rolled down the hill, huh?"

"No, I took it off and brought it up here. I put it over the smokestack," he says. "You two are so cool, you just think something burned on the stove. This whole goddamned tent is filled with smoke because I've got a coffee can on the chimney. And you guys just run around here and open this, and open that, and pull this . . . you haven't slowed down yet. I had the best joke and you guys screwed it up!"

So that night we got into town. A lot of times the guests [and packers] will, if they have time, all go out for dinner. These guys were going to still be in town that night, so we went to Sam's Place for dinner. We all put our orders in.

I slipped out into the dining room and saw this great big rock that was being used as a door jam. I picked it up and took it in the kitchen. I said to the waitress, "I'd like you to serve this big rock to that man." I said pointing to the joker, "When it's time to put his dinner down, I just want you to set this down in front of him."

Now, she weren't too sure about this, but okay, she said, they'd do it.

So when it was time to serve the dinners, here she comes out. She had that rock on a platter with white doilies underneath it and garnish all around—parsley and tomatoes, all this business. She set it down in front of him. The look on this man's face when he saw that he was getting a rock . . . he just started laughing.

Jim [Marva's husband] thought it looked like a cantaloupe and couldn't figure out why the guy would order a whole cantaloupe.

"You really got me this time," the joker said.

I looked over at him. "You've only been in town two hours and you've already pissed another cook off." (1995)

Marva gets the better laugh in the story's second half, because the participants all understand and are comfortable with the joking dynamics. This is not the case in the first half of the story. An unidentified prankster, referred to as "a man," "the man," or "the joker" but someone who is definitely a tourist, takes the coffee can normally used to store toilet paper and puts it atop the stovepipe of the cook tent, causing it to fill with smoke. He then waits for the female staff's response, which will be the payoff for his playful prank. What he doesn't anticipate is that there will be no reaction at all. A look at the situation explains why. To begin with, the camp stoves, which resemble large, flat, rusty tin cans and which Marva notes "aren't pretty but do the job," smoke even when there's not a coffee can on the stovepipe. Second, and most importantly, because the packers and cooks must meet the trucks and horse trailers at a specific time to insure the boss doesn't have to pay overtime for his pickup crew, the last morning of camp is always busy. Marva and her helper, Anita, are oblivious to the smoke because they're in a hurry, or because they assume that it's caused by all of the rushed cooking they're doing to get breakfast served and cleaned up. They're working.

As a result, the joker/guest sees that his intended prank isn't recognized and comes in to explain it—always an admission of failure, though often provoked by the prankster's sense of superiority in the face of the target's ignorance. Now clearly, the guest doesn't understand the busy fury of the last morning of camp, nor does he seem familiar with the habits of a tin stove. (Or as women who cook, perhaps, Anita and Marva are simply more familiar with and resistant to smoke, which the joker has a hard time withstanding.) Such understanding is essential for successful joking, as Mahadev Apte explains: "Familiarity with a cultural code is a prerequisite for the spontaneous mental restructuring of elements that results in amusement and laughter or for the recognition of such restructuring in the sociocultural reality" (1985,

16–17). Or as Gregory Bateson puts it, "play can only occur when participants are capable of some degree of metacommunication, i.e. exchange of signals which carry the message 'this is play'" (1972, 187).[4] In "Pissing Off the Cook," what we have is a failure to metacommunicate. The guest doesn't understand the cultural or work codes within which Marva and Anita function, nor do the women recognize the guest's signals of play. Why exactly does the joke fail? Leaving aside the obvious answer that the tourist's attempt to smoke out Marva and Anita isn't funny—they are inhaling smoke, after all—I would suggest that the tourist's threatening or disturbing behavior is not translated into play, or even recognized at all, precisely because the women are at work. In Bateson's terms the play bite is a real bite, but not for Marva or Anita, who never acknowledge the "bite," or threat. It is the jokester himself who is "bitten" by the smoke, which, while annoying, still doesn't impede Marva or Anita's progress.

In short Marva has other things on her mind, and one of the most striking qualities of her narrative is its self-reflectivity, both in the actions of the protagonist and in the movements of the narrative itself.[5] Marva does a lot of thinking out loud about what she did or might have done. When telling the tale's first half, she seems to be talking to herself, almost reminding herself of things that she must have thought. When she runs down to the outhouse and discovers the toilet paper missing, for instance, she dismisses the fact, figuring it's "no big deal" as they are leaving that morning anyway. As her audience, I found myself drawn into this process as well. "You know," she reminds me, how smoky tents get "if you burn bacon," and with phrases like "so anyway" she continually acknowledges to me and herself that she needs to get back to her set narrative. In much the same way, as a busy camp worker on the last morning of the job, it is Marva's responsibility to keep things moving, regardless of minor mysteries or inconveniences. A little smoke will not stop her, and while she takes all the appropriate safety measures, opening up the tent windows and flaps, she simply doesn't have the luxury of thinking that someone is playing with her.

In the second half of the story, Marva not only tops the joker's failed prank, but also teaches him about the suitable times for conducting actual play. Marva's joking relationship with the guests in this episode certainly contains aggression,

Lynn Breaky-Clark (*left*) and Marva Mountjoy (*right*) in Lynn's kitchen, 2000.
Photograph courtesy of Karen Cowdrey

in part because of the rock's symbolism as the original weapon, but because
the participants recognize it as a joke, all can have a good laugh. Creatively
attacking, Marva triumphs over the guest, which even he admits, by topping
his joke. Stylistically, this section is less rambling and introspective, almost as
if this part has been rehearsed many times, framed in a more cohesive, eco-
nomical structure. Part of the joke's success depends on its public performance,
since the entire community gets to share in the laugh. Sam's Place[6] and Three-
Finger Jack's are the two restaurants in Winthrop where Claude Miller, Marva's
employer, and Marva entertain their guests. Familiar with the relaxed atmosphere of these final dinners, it's not surprising that the staff at Sam's would
willingly help Marva with her prank, and especially when they know she will
take responsibility for any bad consequences. In fact, through the elaborate presentation of the rock, the employees at Sam's also get in on the laugh.

Marva had a good laugh telling this story—and I should mention that she
actually enjoys this joker's type of play. Perhaps to insure that I didn't have

a negative impression of the jokester, after Marva told me "Pissing Off the Cook" she told me another story about him. In the summer of 1994, she took that same guest on a pack trip. The whole time, she warned him teasingly to stay out of her kitchen for fear he'd try and trick her again. One day, Marva took some other guests on a fishing trip to a nearby lake. The joker stayed in camp. She returned to find her kitchen, set up exactly as it had been in her mess tent, sitting in the middle of a meadow some distance from camp. Taking the kitchen out bit by bit, the joking guest had ridden it on horseback about a mile over to the new site so that when Marva rode through the meadow she could have a proper laugh. Marva's clear enjoyment of this scene when recalling the jokester's efforts makes it clear that she and the jokester are, in this case, on the same wavelength. Trust has been established—the real bite has been transformed into a play bite.

In the next story that Marva told as a humorous tale, "A High Ol' Time," she experiences uneasy play. This story is more threatening and potentially violent than "Pissing Off the Cook," and the dynamics of the teller/audience relationship are far more complicated. The tale describes a pack trip that involves drugs, sexual harassment, uneasy play, and Marva's personal empowerment.

A High Ol' Time

We were going to someplace called Sheep Mountain. Well, since I had gone on the Oval Lakes [pack trip] before, I knew this was going to be a piece of cake. You don't have to do anything—just ride along with the packer. Well, now, we're on a whole new program.

Unbeknownst to me, when you have a guest riding, the cook is in charge and is responsible for getting off the trailhead to where the camp is. Well, I didn't think to look at a map. I mean we're going to Sheep Mountain, surely everything's all labeled. Besides, I thought the people would be riding with Claude on this trip. It wasn't till we got to the cowboy breakfast at Jack's [Three-Finger Jack's Restaurant] that Claude told me he couldn't go and that I'd have to pack the group in with Tyler. I had five guys to pack up to the mountains. They were young men from all over the country: They gathered once a year—college buddies—and they went on a trip together—professionals—twenty-two or twenty-three, something like that.

Anyway, there we go. There's no signs as to where I'm supposed to go. Well, I started up. Of course, I make the first wrong turn and Tyler catches me. That's who I'd gotten to pack—Tyler. He gets me back on the right road and he gets in front of me. So then I'm watching where Tyler's going. I don't read the tracks real well, so I'd ride up real fast to make sure Tyler was still in front of me and try to take care of the guests.

What I was getting to, I guess, was that I didn't realize that I was going to be responsible for these guests, and taking care of them. You have to, ya know, pick up fourteen hundred things off the trail. You have to tie all the horses up. When you've got a bunch [of guests] . . . when you have two or three, that's a piece of cake—but when you've got a half a dozen or more of them, it's a pain in the neck. You're just like a yo-yo—up and down.

And you never want to stop on the trail, because if you stop that's when you're going to get in trouble. If you keep them moving on the horses, you're safe. But the minute they want to stop and take a picture (I'll let the horse drink and dangle the reins), there are all these things that can happen. If you keep them moving on the horse, then you're safe.

Well, I went ahead. I was having trouble because these guys just wouldn't keep up with me. And I, of course, was panicking because I didn't know where I was supposed to go, so I wanted to go fast enough to keep up with the packer. Well, that wasn't working, but I was loping ahead and coming back. Finally, I said something to them because I could see they were like sneaking cigarettes back there. I said, "It's all right if you smoke on the trail but listen, it's too dry. You can't drop any cigarette butts because it's completely against the rules. You know, put your cigarette out and put the butt in your pocket. Be careful and it's okay. Let's keep up," I told them.

Well, they just weren't keeping up. So I went back to check on them, kind of waited for them, and all of a sudden I smelled all these wonderful wildflowers. God, it was just a beautiful smell and the colors were beautiful. And, all of a sudden it dawned on me—this is not cigarettes; this is not wildflowers. Oh gosh! It was! And, they were having quite a high ol' time.

I didn't get into camp until like eight o'clock that night. I just could not make them go. Well, they proceeded through the week—it's the only time I've had a drug problem on any of the trips I've ever been on.

One day, they decided they wanted to stay in camp and they were playing cards and they were drinking, and of course, they had their marijuana in their little baggies.

And then, they were gone somewhere, and while they were gone, I guess I didn't realize what was in those little baggies at that time, because I was cleaning up and tidying up around the campfire and I threw those bags in and they kept the campfire burning.

Boy, they came back and they were just beside themselves. First, they didn't tell me what I had burned but they were beside themselves. Then, I realized what it was. But, they had lots of it, I guess, because they got some more out. They were still quite happy characters.

Then, one night Tyler took the horses out to graze. So, I was left in camp alone with them. And, from the looks of these guys, and I had never been around drugs enough to know, but the eyes and the way they were acting . . . and well, they kind of patted me on the butt. I said to myself, oh, I don't think I feel real safe right here, right now. Because, I thought, they've been drinking and they've got their drugs or whatever. I don't know if they was popping pills—*they* just didn't, well, *it* didn't look good.

So I decided that I better get out of camp. I took a book and slipped out when they weren't watching. Then, I had a real hard talk, a long talk with myself, and decided I could outride these guys. All I had to do was turn their horses loose and get on my horse and ride away. I didn't have to stay and put up with any of this stuff. Once I made that decision in my own mind, I never have had a problem with any of the guests. It was just that one time. I guess I had to grow up and learn that this is what to do if you ever get in a spot that you're uncomfortable with. You know, I never had that problem again.

We came out on that trip and those guys were still slow riding out. I knew they were still using their marijuana. They were lagging. I thought, my God, we'll never get out. Claude's guys are going to get to the trailhead to meet us and have the trucks ready. They're going to want us at five o'clock and we're not going to be there. Finally, I told the guys that my husband was going to meet us and he'd bring us beer to the trailhead, which sometimes they do if they bring the trucks up. I told them he was a law enforcement officer and he would be at the trailhead.

It was like a miracle! Those guys could keep up. You can't believe how fast those horses could walk. It worked! They put it away and they peddled on out of there. (1995)

Apart from Marva herself, "A High Ol' Time" has no round, developed characters. The vaguely described young professional men start off lumped together with other kinds of tourists. What eventually makes them distinctive is that they smoke pot and they won't listen to Marva. The second trait is more significant than it might appear. After taking three separate pack trips with Marva, I found it hard to believe that there were people who didn't listen to her. Almost six feet tall, she's verbally direct and a formidable, even intimidating presence. Certainly, she's very present in the telling. To a far greater degree than even in "Pissing Off the Cook," in this acutely self-evaluating story Marva is continually articulating her reflections, uncertainties, and fears. Even more importantly, these digressions are set out as momentary diversions from the main narrative, which is supposedly a funny story about work. Verbal signs such as "Anyway, there we go," "What I was getting to," and the repeated word "Well" explicitly nudge the audience away from dialogue with the teller and back into the narrative proper.

Bakhtin usefully describes the dynamics of this sense of double play commonly found in narrative:

> Before us are two events—the event that is narrated in the work and the event of narration itself (we ourselves participate in the latter, as listeners or readers); these events take place in different times (which are marked by different durations as well) and in different places, but at the same time these two events are indissolubly united in a single but complex event that we might call the work in the totality of all its events, including the external material evenness of the work, and its text, and the world represented in the text, and the author/creator and the listener or reader; thus we perceive the fullness of the work in all its wholeness and indivisibility, but at the same time we understand the diversity of the elements that constitute it. (1981, 255)

Bahktin not only implicates the listening audience in the construction of meaning, but also notes that language within a single story can shift its temporal and judgmental coordinates. In terms of the listening audience, Babcock stresses "the relationship which exists between the narrator and his audience vis-à-vis a narrative message." Two types of frames, external and internal, structure this relationship. The internal frame, which in Marva's case is the sequence of events for this specific trip, is the ostensibly funny story. The external frame is "the performance, specific reference made to the performance, the audience, the message, the code, the channel or medium of expression, the register, etc., or any combination thereof"—in short, the telling itself, which in Marva's case is heavily conditioned by sexual and power politics and by contemporary tourist culture as embedded in the community of Winthrop, with its unspoken but powerful expectations of her (Babcock 1978, 66).

What is immediately apparent about the internal structure is that in terms of shared humor, there is nothing funny about the situation. Nothing takes place that Marva or her employers, the tourists, jointly recognize as joking or play. In fact, unlike the joker in "Pissing Off the Cook," these tourists at first seem totally uninterested in what Marva might be thinking or doing. Reckless, inexperienced, and drugged, the young professionals represent a mass of undisciplined tourists who ignore the rules and by their lawless behavior place a great deal of pressure on their packers. In this sense the men fit the stereotype of wealthy but dumb greenhorns or tourists—precisely the figures that cowboy culture would consider worthy targets for practical jokes or suitable clowns for humorous anecdotes and tall tales. These figures are cartoons to the teller's culture—representatives of contemporary urban society who have no respect for the wilderness or cowboy culture.

As Marva's story points out, however, butts of this kind have been and continue to be very dangerous to western or cowboy culture. The problem arises from the difference between the mythic cowboy and the very real packer. As Dary notes, in his ideal form: "The cowboy symbolizes the free life, closely tied to the out-of-doors and Nature. The impact of land, the grass, the rivers and streams and gushing springs, the color of the sky and the clouds, the climates and the weather—these things are characteristic of the real and the mythical cowboy cultures" (1989, 338). Whether or not the real cowboy felt this "mythical" connection with nature, however, is questionable. The actual cowboy was often someone working for a minimal salary in a job for which he needed no formal education; generally he was an uneducated drifter, frequently from the eastern United States. Big business in the form of cattle-centered markets soon put an end to the truly self-determining cowboy. As any cultural historian knows, "the man in business and industry, deeply rooted in the East" was largely responsible for destroying the rugged, natural western culture during the nineteenth century. Even today, Dary notes, "the business culture that now stretches from the Atlantic to the Pacific still believes in the mythical culture created by its writers, and too many Americans are shaping their lives after images of that mythical culture, one that never existed" (1989, 338).

Though in retrospect Marva could not remember what kind of professionals these men were, and though she herself has a college degree in social work, the tourists' status and behavior certainly matches the arrogant, inconsiderate, and willful profile that western culture often recognizes in the highly educated outsider. And while this outsider can be a target for tall tales, she is also indisputably a figure who wields economic authority. Marva, in short, is leading a group of outsiders who feel they can do anything they want because they are in the West, in the wilderness, and in the role of customers or employers. Compounding the problem for Marva is her status as a horsewoman within the western community itself. She is clearly annoyed, though in a muted way, at her boss for failing to inform her that he will not be accompanying her. Apparently, Claude Miller didn't notify Marva of this change until the morning of the pack trip, leaving her in charge of leading the tourists to the camp. Since she had assumed that things would be the same as on a previous trip, when Claude was riding along, Marva had not taken the time to read the maps and familiarize herself totally with the area. Nor does Tyler, the packer, provide much support, riding so far ahead that for navigating purposes he might as well not be there. Marva's initial challenge, therefore, is simply to keep her guests on track and moving, without ever letting them know she is uncertain or concerned. Initially, her attempts are quite funny in a self-mocking way; her account of comic attempts to keep her packer in sight by charging up and down the trail struck me as similar to the frantic activity of a Tom and Jerry cartoon. While the images are presented comically in the narration and the narrative, however, Marva's urgency as she rides back and forth has a professional dimension as well—she takes things very seriously. Knowing her firsthand, it seemed almost impossible to me that Marva could lose control of a situation involving packing and guests. This potential for losing authority increases as the story moves forward, giving it what tension and suspense it possesses.

At first the dynamics are those of the typical western fantasy pack trip: while the guests are actively enjoying their adventure, Marva is tending to her professional responsibilities, which include letting her charges just play. The only reason, after all, that they need to keep moving is Marva's own awareness that she is not prepared. Nor are the drugs immediately presented as ominous or dangerous. Marva never actually tells her guests that she is distressed by their marijuana smoking, probably because she feels it is none of her business as long as they are not directly bothering her with it. She does, however, instruct them about their cigarettes, since they represent a fire hazard. At certain moments she even seems to find the subject amusing, as when she describes her own realization that they are smoking dope or when she hints that she herself felt the smoke was affecting her—certainly a comic exaggeration, since she is riding in a wide-open area. Marva trivializes her concern about the situation through her use of self-mockery. Radner explains, "Like other strategies of coding, trivialization (particularly through humor) can buffer the acerbity of the message not only for the audience but also for the performer herself" (1993, 20). But her guests' intoxication seriously threatens Marva's ability to maintain her authority as a horsewoman, and she sets out to eliminate the threat. Almost excessively, she explains and justifies what she felt she had to do as part of her job. Particularly interesting, however, is the way she adopts a traditional woman's role to carry out her plan. She says she quickly realized her guests were smoking pot but then expects her audience to believe that she didn't realize the little baggies she threw in the campfire (supposedly to keep it going!) contain the marijuana. In the wilderness, though, this strategy succeeds. The guests are "beside themselves" when they discover what she's done, but they cannot really complain, since to do so would be to admit their illegal activity, which there is at least a chance Marva is oblivious to. She therefore resorts at first to a classic submissive strategy, a passive-aggressive throwing of the marijuana into the fire that leaves her actual intention blurry to the guests, though quite clear, and humorous, to her listening audience—me.

The guests, however, apparently have more pot, for they are "still quite happy characters," and soon Marva is dealing with a far more serious threat to her authority. When the guests start "playing" with Marva, patting her butt, she perceives it as a very dangerous sign. Her sense of concern has a number of sources. First, and a factor that should not be taken lightly, is her strong sense of propriety. Marva shares with her community a strong concern about the way things look. Toward the end of her interview, she told me that one of her role models was her mother-in-law, a "lady" who taught her about hostessing and polite reserve. Second, Marva recognizes that the freedom from restraint the wilderness promises might suggest situations that the guests would pursue there though nowhere else or that a simple change of gender could make acceptable, and even funny, for the packers themselves. Clearly, the guests do not realize the discomfort they have caused Marva, seeing her perhaps as a "pard,"[7] a good old girl who will welcome their advances. As for the issue of tourist/packer sex on the trail, when I asked Marva if male packers ever had similar experiences with harassment in the wilderness, she called one over.

"Hey Rod," she yelled as he trotted up, "what do you call it when women come onto you on pack trips."

Rod laughed, "Well, Claude calls that fringe benefits."

This obvious difference in attitude toward advances by tourists—the male community considering it play and a perk of the job, the female community considering it a threat and a denial of women's authority—points to Marva's third and perhaps most troubling concern: her worry that she has lost control professionally. The intimidation of violence through rape threatens Marva as a woman and a horsewoman, even to the point of suggesting that situations like this show why women should not be on the trail at all: she is in the wilderness with five stoned and threatening men, with the packer out with the horses and no one else there to protect her. Furthermore, within her own and many other communities, there is still at least some sentiment that as a woman, the very fact that she let herself get into this situation suggests that she almost deserves the consequences. For Marva, then, unchecked sexual advances not only represent a physical danger, but a threat to her standing in the community and her job.

Small wonder that after the patting Marva leaves camp with a book and has a "real hard talk" with herself. Within the chivalric Code of the West, the packer, her boss, or her husband would presumably avenge Marva's honor. But at the moment of the guests' transgression none of these protecting figures happen to be around, and Marva realizes that she will have to think of something else. Personal violence in self-defense? Although Marva's ability to be aggressive has already been demonstrated by the burning of the dope, actual violence doesn't seem to occur to her, even though packers typically carry guns on these trips (she once told me, "just in case"). Instead, without violence against the transgressors or dependence on male rescue or protection, Marva draws on the power of her professional experience. The solution to her dilemma, should the guests continue with their unruly behavior, is to let their horses loose, get on her horse, and ride away, a solution that arises from her own confidence in herself as a packer/cook/scout. In short, by not retreating when faced with the potential sexual threat but instead exhibiting courage, independence, and individuality through her choice to remain in the camp, Marva modifies that essential cowboy trait of self-reliance and in the process enters, on her own terms, into the Code of the West.

The most obvious invocations of the Code here have to do with the sources of cowboy strength—though with a difference. First, Marva draws on power that is personal and rests upon her knowledge of horses and the wilderness—the ground for western survival. Second, she takes personal responsibility for dealing with an insult. No one else can fight a real cowboy's battles for him, and by not only personally tossing the marijuana into the fire, but also refusing to threaten vengeance from other men like her husband or the packer, Marva asserts her own authority as a horsewoman. But third, and most interesting for my purposes, at the key moment Marva gratifies herself without actually having to display her strength or knowledge overtly. Now certainly, a number of explanations for this could be suggested. The most macho would be that the truly competent individual does not need to demonstrate her abilities. Those whose opinions matter simply *know*. A second possibility would fit in with the tall-tale tradition: the tenderfoot or outsider, by his very ignorance, is never actually aware that he has been ridiculed or humiliated by a master. In this narrative one-upmanship remains hidden until the story is told, and the contempt for the outsider only appears in the story's telling, since the tourists themselves are never aware of Marva's observations. The narrative's tall-tale dimension of humiliating the tenderfoot is only witnessed by the outsider/listener—me. As such a listener, I am personally embarrassed by the behavior of these young men, for while I am not sympathetic, I understand their lack of control as tourists. Presumably, then, my role in this narration will be to share with the outside community those elements of the tale that illustrate inappropriate behavior in the wilderness.

As Marva's audience, I also receive a lesson on personal empowerment. The next important reason for Marva's apparent inaction is probably economic. As a tourist-dependent community, Winthrop cannot afford confrontations with its source of income. After her "real hard talk," then, Marva knows that she is definitely in control; she does not explicitly announce this. The guests continue their behavior, and only Marva and the listener know that things have changed, that Marva has gained the upper hand. This personal triumph also occurs despite Marva's status as a woman within the Winthrop community and within the tradition of the West. It is not just the tourists who ignore or underestimate her, but the dominant male western community as well. As a result Marva's narrative is a critical revision of the humorous stories told by men in cowboy culture, a revision that culture might not understand or accept. The story's climax comes when Marva decides to do nothing—yet. Furthermore, she makes a virtue of enjoying her triumph without ever letting her victims know, a secret one-upmanship that at the very least leaves the confrontational assumptions of the western tradition open to some interrogation. Further supporting my reading here is Marva's easy return to conventional humorous narrative in her throwaway joke about the ride back. As I've mentioned, Marva could have revealed that her husband was a law-enforcement officer when her guests were patting her on the butt, but she chose not to, leaving the tourists unaware of what potentially awaits them if they misbehave with her again. Only when she's on her way back to the trailhead, firmly in control in her own mind but with her charges still smoking and poking along, does Marva bring up her husband—a game warden in the Methow Valley—and even then she sweetens the threat with a promise of beer. This too is a victory of sorts. Knowing that she has professional control over the situation, she can relax into taking advantage of her stereotyped role as a woman to get her guests moving.

But in all of this, where is the joke? As Mary Douglas notes, "any recognizable joke falls into a pattern in need of two elements, the juxtaposition of a control against that which is controlled, this juxtaposition being such that the latter triumphs." In Marva's case the story's exhibition of control versus lack of control only takes place in the telling, but it nevertheless enacts that dramatic shift Douglas describes: "a successful subversion of one form by another completes or ends the joke, for it changes the balance of power" (1975, 96). Radner's description of distraction as a feminist narrative strategy also helps to account for the curious nonevent climax in Marva's tale. Radner describes distractions as "Strategies that drown out or draw attention away from the subversive power of a feminist message." Even more pointedly for my purposes, "Usually distraction involves creating some kind of 'noise,' interference, or obscurity that will keep the message from being heard except by those who listen very carefully or already suspect it is there (1993, 15). In Marva's tale her many changes and frantic activity, as well as her laughter and self-mocking tone, conceal or lighten what is actually the brutally simple story of a woman feeling threatened. Further, all this verbal and dramatic activity stands in sharp contrast to her unchanging, inflexible guests, flat characters rigidly and comically defined by stereotypical tourist and male behavior. They represent that power which many theorists of women's humor claim must shift to the woman for a joke to occur. Gloria Kaufman explains how humor changes its meaning, depending on its location in social power dynamics:

> Humor and power are related in highly complex ways. On the one hand society has recognized the expression (or creation) of humor as an exercise of power and has reacted negatively to women humorists. (Things are changing.) On the other hand, women and other suppressed groups have privately and regularly used humor to empower themselves in order to survive oppression or subversively to resist it. No one doubts that humor is empowering. It is especially positive in dispelling fear. Laughing at our enemies diminishes them and emboldens us. (1991, ix)

These remarks are useful in two ways. By pointing to the relationships between laughter and courage, Kaufman certainly helps to account for Marva's grasping of authority during her talk with herself. In this story Douglas's "balance of power" tips not only when Marva realizes her own expertise, which has been there all along but which she has to take herself aside to rediscover, but also when she realizes that this power of knowledge makes her guests look like incompetent fools. In social terms it is also significant that despite superior knowledge of the wilderness, horses, and tourists, Marva only realizes her power during a moment of crisis late in the story, since she functions within strict rules of propriety regarding the treatment of tourists and because her confidence as a leader has been shaken first by her employer, then by her packer's thoughtlessness, and finally by the behavior of her guests. Her discovery that she has the power and the expertise necessary to transform situations intelligently flies in the face of what she is confronted with in the dominant culture.

Marva announces and explains this empowerment through a humorous narrative that subverts and misdirects the audience at large. But Kaufman's emphasis on the joking group's and individual's often private savoring of a joke is important. Kaufman notes that hearing jokes by women or other subordinates can make dominant groups "grudgingly admit our wit, if only subconsciously, and that somewhat weakens their will to oppress us" and that joking "sometimes nourishes their self-doubts." But Kaufman also suggests that just as often, when they hear our impertinent, fearless humor, it additionally discomfits or angers them" (1991, x), which accounts in part for why so many of the Winthrop horsewomen's stories only become jokes when they are told to me. Both as a woman in a self-consciously western community and as a worker in the tourist economy, Marva must be very careful about whom she pisses off. Most obviously, she decides to keep the guests in the dark, leaving them as humorous targets who believe they have control of a wilderness situation. But because of the hints of sexual threatening, it is also hard to imagine Marva's telling this story as it stands to male packers or to her husband, who might feel obliged either to react violently toward the tourists or, even worse, to limit Marva's further economic participation in the wilderness under the pretense of physical protection. As a result, the issue of audience and, more specifically, the nature of that audience, is central to the horsewoman's joking here.

The relationship between the joke teller, Marva, and the selected audience, me, resembles what Walker describes as the foundation of humor itself. According to Walker, "the humorous vision requires the ability to hold two contradictory realities in suspension simultaneously—to perform a mental balancing act that superimposes a comic version of life on the observable 'facts'" (1988, 82). The teller, Marva, communicates the "facts" by assuming a comic perspective toward them and then shares it with her listeners. As Bauman explains, performance thus creates its own social structure, offering "to the participants a special enhancement of experience bringing with it a heightened intensity of communicative interaction which binds the audience to the performer in a way that is specific to the performance as a mode of communication" (1986, 43). This appeal to, and constituting of, a community outside of the tale takes place in a variety of ways. In Marva's story, though, far more specific conditions influence the complex joke teller–audience relationship. Since only in the telling does Marva's story turn threat into humor, the story must be addressed to an audience who *wishes* the result to be humorous, and who works to put the pieces of Marva's narrative together into something that does shift power.

What is required, then, is a consciousness that can recognize the main lines of the story, and even eventually communicate them, *with Marva's understanding of them,* to an implied larger audience outside of the Winthrop population. In this instance the story is told to a researcher who, if necessary, can play the roles of scholar, friend, woman, cowgirl wanna-be, or tourist. Predictably, the result is not a single "meaning" but an equally diverse, and at times unflattering, set of insights into Marva's social situation and my own. On the positive side, I take from Marva's story the assurance that I am not a victim unless I allow myself to be and that I have knowledge to which other people do not have access. Less comfortingly, I also confront, once more, the subordinate role assumed for me as a woman, not only within my own culture, but also within Marva's community. The story is given in trust as well. I am to carry a message to the community at large that neither drug-related behavior nor inappropriate sexual advances by tourists are appreciated or tolerated by at least one Winthrop horsewoman. Perhaps the hardest lesson, however, turned out to be a retroactive personal chastening. As Marva told her story, I remembered our first pack trip together, when I had asked her to stop a few times so I could take pictures. At the time I was very short on horse sense. Not completely realizing the depth of a horse's pernicious and flighty nature, I chose places with excellent vistas but steep, narrow trails. After completing eight weeks in cowgirl school, I recognized that my wish to document my first wilderness pack trip had led me unknowingly to endanger my family, my packers, and myself.[8] But I had to learn this on my own. As Marva told me about her silent disapproval of her guests on the trail, I thought about how she had never said no to my requests for photographs.

In our society men are urged to stand apart, while women are relegated to a sphere where it is usually better to slip neatly into the fold of other women. Since Walker and many others argue that humorists stand apart from their own reality so they can view it with "detachment and objectivity" (1988, 23), it would seem that humor itself is a kind of hyper-male activity, requiring "a stance of superiority" even more elevated than usual "in order to point out incongruities or absurdity in the world that others are accustomed to accept on its own terms (1988, 25). Individuality, superiority, and aggressiveness—unfeminine qualities all—are therefore the necessary traits of the humorist. But as Marva Mountjoy's stories and others I discuss all demonstrate, humor can demand a very specific social context and a highly idiosyncratic audience—one that, in the case of women's humor, might not include men at all, at least during the initial telling. In both "Pissing Off the Cook" and "A High Ol' Time," then, Marva's refusal to respond to male joking or aggression might be not only a sign of professional activity and authority, but also a subtle protest, shared later with a chosen audience, against the dominant male, western, and tourist cultures that exploit her.

Experts in the field of cowboy humor reinforce women's invisibility. West explains the role of women in the American West this way: "Such a paragon of virtue hardly provides subject matter for humor. The woman, as has been noted earlier, was generally elevated to a point of reverence by the cowboy. But there were times when the individual woman did not live up to the idea. It was then that she provided the laughter, but not often was the laughter smutty or demeaning" (1990, 86). I suspect that whether or not the joke is "smutty or demeaning" would often depend on the audience. In his study of cowboy humor, Stan Hoig calls women "scarcer than 'clean socks in a bunkhouse'" (1958, 76). Both West and Hoig suggest that when pondering cowboy humor, most writers think of women as objects and subjects of jokes rather than as the tellers. Certainly this reading conforms to typical representations of women in cowboy culture, in which ranch women, wearing flour sacks for dresses and untied lace-up shoes, are comic butts. In cowboy humor, frontier ranch women are often depicted as vain, stupid, and illogical—the targets, as Roach points out, of jokes, stories, and tall tales, "none of them gentle" (1990, 103).

In *The Cowgirls* Roach describes one of Lex Graham's best cartoons, which features the helpful wife. It shows both husband and wife riding after a steer. The husband ropes the steer and the wife, with a satisfied smile, ropes the hind legs of her husband's horse. One reading of the cartoon might be that the helpful wife is smiling stupidly over her success at roping her husband's horse, stunningly oblivious, apparently, to the danger she has put him in.

But another reading of the cartoon would focus on the wife's delight that not only has she successfully roped an animal, but also that it is her husband's horse. The violent end her husband will suffer in a moment, when he flies off that horse only to be dragged behind the charging steer, has that roughhouse, radical, and satisfying appeal that slapstick or visual humor often supplies. But for women, of course, responding this way to such a cartoon, especially when the knocked-about buffoon is a male, has been traditionally judged a violation of those cultural norms that define ladylike behavior. Since even laughing out loud can be condemned as unruly, women's irreverent humor is usually whispered or presented as somehow innocently directed at its male targets, and often its male audience. Humor theorist Walker explains:

> The humorist is at odds with the publicly espoused values of the culture, over-turning its sacred cows, pointing out the nakedness of not only the emperor, but also the politician, the pious and the pompous. For women to adopt this role means that they must break out of the passive, subordinate position mandated for them by centuries of patriarchal tradition and take on the power accruing to those who reveal the shams, hypocrisies, and incongruities of the dominant culture. (1988, 9)

Following this line of thought, Kathleen Rowe concludes that "the unruly women who have laughed in such ways, or have wanted to—might help loosen the bitter hold of those social and cultural structures that for centuries have tried to repress it" (1995, 2–3). As for the subversive nature of women's humor, Carol Mitchell argues that "Women also tell a higher percentage of jokes involving death to males than to any other audience, which may further indicate that females use jokes as aggressive conduct toward males" (1985, 184). Graham's cartoon gathers together three of the components that interest me most in the humorous discourse of women in the Methow Valley: the woman's undeniable expertise and physical competence; her aggressive, even violent capacity for subversion and rebellion; and the covering or masking smile.

For example, consider the following story told by Judy Mally-Burkhart, who considered it one of her funniest.

A WELL-BROKE MULE

We were on a pack trip up to the Pasayten at about six thousand feet. Our routine starts early—about five o'clock. We wrangled the horses. We were taking the guests to a lake to fish and sightsee. We had twelve horses to get ready that morning—I was catching, brushing, and saddling the horses and helping the people get on their horses. I also was giving a mini–riding lesson. I made sure that everything was secure and that their [the guests'] saddlebags had their lunches in them. Frank Kline was helping us wrangle that morning.

We have a lot of bay mules that look alike. So Frank wrangled them and got them all tied up in the area. We usually put all the mules down at one end of the line and all the saddle horses at the other. The riding mules go up with the horses. So Frank caught 'em and brushed them and I went around and threw the saddles on 'em and cinched them up. Then Mary Yaken, the other wrangler, came along and bridled 'em.

We had our breakfast and the guests got on the horses and started getting ready to take off. I put one man on Fred, a mule. The guy was an inexperienced rider, but I knew that Fred was a well-broke mule. He is like a Cadillac. He's really smooth—a good mule.

The man said, "My saddle's coming forward."

"I'll pull it back," I said. Well, it felt like the mule hunched. I looked at him and Fred hunched. "I'll fix your saddle."

The guest jumped off while I readjusted the saddle, then I had him climb back on. The next thing I knew, Fred headed off for the picket line with the rest of the mules, like he didn't want to work.

My husband [Aaron Lee] saw Fred. "I think Fred must need a tune-up," he said. "I'll ride him."

The guest got off and Aaron Lee jumped on the mule. Fred started bucking. Everybody was gathered around and watching. It's quite an experience to see a mule bucking.

"Ride 'em, honey," I yelled. Aaron Lee was getting nowhere because Fred was still bucking.

"I need my spurs," he said.

I ran up to Aaron Lee's saddled horse and grabbed his spurs out of his saddle-bag.

He put 'em on and jumped back onto Fred. He was really working Fred over and Fred was spinning in circles, just bucking like crazy. And the guests—well, their eyes were open wide like they couldn't believe it. They were getting a rodeo in the middle of the wilderness. Fred was bucking so hard that the saddle was flying up over his head. Aaron Lee decided to get off.

"Well, I'm not going to ride him," he said. "Boy, I sure wish I had a bridging. This saddle won't stay on. If I had a briching, I'd ride him all the way to the lake. By God, that'd make him go."

A briching goes down the back and under the tail. Some bridging goes all the way around the back legs like a harness.

So we got the guest another horse to ride. We usually have a spare horse in case one gets lame. We rotate horses around on a long trip with that many people. Aaron Lee tied Fred up in the picket line and we went to the lake.

When we got back Aaron Lee says, "Did somebody move Fred?"

"No," said Ann Harvey, the camp cook, "I didn't move 'im."

"Well, how come he's standing in a different place?" Aaron Lee was talking about John.

I had saddled John instead of Fred.

John had never had anybody on his back, his whole life. Here was this guest who was an amateur greenhorn who was on a mule who had never had anybody on his back. And there's John. When he saw us riding up, he started saying "ooooooooooh." Mules talk to you. The corners of his mouth were sore from Aaron Lee trying to ride him. Oh God, it was so funny.

And there's Fred, as happy as could be standing there. He hadn't had to work that day. I asked Mary how in the world she got the bridle with a bit on John. "I sweet-talked him for about a half hour," she said.

Aaron Lee teased me relentlessly about how I tried to kill him by saddling the wrong mule. (2000)

I first interviewed Judy in 1992 in her saddle shop: Early Winters Saddle and Leather Shop. Afterward, she drove me down to her house (a short distance down the road) to watch her horse drill-team videos. A group of young women staged an impressive performance on horseback around a corral twirling flags on poles. Judy has ridden horses since she was four years old, growing up in the Midwest. She came to the Methow Valley with a friend. She said that she loved the mountains so much she stayed. Like Lauralee Northcott, she also married into a family with Methow Valley pioneer heritage. Having lived in the valley over twenty-five years, she works with her husband running Early Winters Outfitters and breeding mules. Judy is also a painter and a saddle maker. She learned to tool leather several years ago and has made a number of saddles. Lauralee Northcott, Kit McLean Cramer, and Virginia Bennett all wear leather chaps created by Judy. One would not call Judy Mally-Burkhart aggressive. Many people have described her as sweet, kind—one of the nicest people in the valley. She would never intentionally saddle an "unbroke" mule for a guest. Yet she finds this experience particularly humorous. Judy giggled when she recalled the mule's violent bucking as Aaron Lee was flying over his head, trying to hang on just like a rodeo rider on a bucking bronco. The tourist audience stood in awe of the show. The guest who managed to get off "Fred" probably thought he was pretty lucky. At the beginning of the story, it seems that Frank Kline was the one responsible for saddling the wrong mule—but later the audience discovers it was actually Judy. Judy is an expert with mules: she breeds, births, and trains mules. Yet the listening audience must suspend her disbelief that Judy could have gotten it wrong. But in some ways admitting that it was her responsibility and that the enjoyment she received watching Aaron Lee's unsuccessful "tune-up" gives her much pleasure in the telling. Obviously, she had no intention of trying to hurt her husband, and yet she seems tickled that it almost happened.

An analysis of who serves as the excluded or scapegoated figure in these women's tales also suggests some interesting modifications that could be made to narrative paradigms. Two targets tend to emerge. First, and most predictably under the circumstances, since the horsewomen's narratives necessarily encompass such themes as sexual harassment, identity, and mediation as well as variously gendered joking relationships in the American West, the resulting stories are often subversive and even aggressive belittlings of men. Though women are not expected to respond to the more reactive dimensions of cowboy culture, their awareness of their unacknowledged but substantial contribution to the formation of the American West often leads them to assert their claims, within these dynamics at least implicitly pushing men from their sole possession of the forefront. But another excluded figure or scapegoat also figures within the horsewomen's stories, one produced not by gender or proximity but by economics and the image of the American West itself. As individuals making a living in a tourist culture, it only makes sense that horsewomen would also use humor and the tall tale to set themselves apart, as experts, from the tourist; in fact, given a cultural environment that denies female ability, claims of authority made through humor and narrative would be more likely to come from women, whether they are addressing men within that environment or outsiders.

Winthrop actively lures tourists not only through the visual beauty of the landscape and the available recreational activities, but also through the town's deliberate western motif. Winthrop often succeeds. Like the cowboy wanna-bes in the film *City Slickers*, tourists can pay a cattleman to let them work for him, thereby presumably having an authentic cowboy experience. And yet, while heartily encouraged to visit Winthrop as visitors, tourists remain marginalized. Nor is it easy to shake that outsider label. I had, of course, noticed that some people in the Winthrop area seemed standoffish—understandable in a small community. But it was only after I became more involved in com-

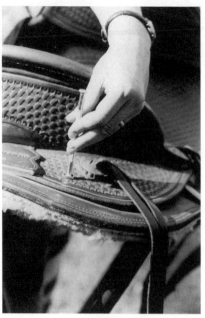

Judy's leather shop, 2005 (*left*), and
Judy Mally-Burkhart, 2000 (*right*).
Photographs courtesy of Karen Cowdrey

munity activities and, even more importantly, only after I cowgirled with Kit
McLean Cramer that I recognized just how excluded visitors and tourists are.

Determined to learn more about cowboy/horsewoman culture, in the summer of 1995 I took riding lessons from Kit. For my first session I wore mascara, jeans, cowboy boots, a nice T-shirt, and what I thought was a cowboy hat—dark green felt with an embroidered band. Kit made fun of my makeup and clothes right away. After that, I knew better than to arrive at the corral too "duded up," so for the next lesson I didn't wear eye makeup and I borrowed one of my husband's denim shirts. But I still had on my green felt hat. Kit noticed: "Looks like you should be hooking flies onto that hat," she said quietly. The lessons themselves proved to be hard, dirty work. After teaching me some basic riding skills, by the second lesson Kit had me catching, saddling, and bridling reluctant trail horses—and let me emphasize the word *reluctant*. After showing me once how to catch a horse, Kit left me in the corral with fifteen loose ones. With the halter dragging behind my back, I sneaked up behind an animal and then slipped the halter over its nose. "Pretend you're giving them a hug," Kit yelled from her bench near the corral. After I pulled the first horse over to the hitching post and tied him up, Kit showed me how to bridle. With the horse's mouth in one hand and the bridle spread out in the other, she said, "Now just shove your thumb right behind the last tooth and slip that bit into his mouth." Although I was sure my thumb would be nipped off, I saddled and bridled seven horses. At the end of a full day of riding, though, as I stood there covered with horse shit, horse slobber, and dirt, Kit told the guests scheduled to go out for an afternoon horseback ride that I was a wrangler. Wanna-be that I was, I was still proud. Simply being around Kit as she carried out her duties sharpened my awareness of how humor functioned within this scene.

Take, for example, the following joking event. What I have entitled "Roasting the Guest" was told to a group of people at Sun Mountain Lodge. Present were Kit, three hotel guests, two wranglers, the employee joke teller, her daughter, her sister, and myself. We stood in the tiny tack room of the stable, north of the hotel, waiting for a rain shower to pass before going on a horseback ride. Though ostensibly telling the joke privately to her sister, the narrator knew that her audience was within earshot.

Roasting the Guest

Hey, Nance, did you hear what happened to that tourist I told you about who complained to each and every department, all week long?

"No."

Well, yesterday was the last straw.

"What happened?"

A lightbulb went out in his room. He yelled at housekeeping for using cheap lightbulbs.

"Gads."

Yeah, so yesterday afternoon, he got a call to come up to the front desk so the staff could deal with his complaints. So he gets to the front desk and no one's there so he starts banging on the bell. You know. BING! BING! BING! BING! "Where is everybody!" he was yelling.

All of a sudden, six employees stand up from behind the front desk, point their rifles, and blast him.

"Geez."

After shooting him, the concierge and security guards came in and dragged him off on a luggage cart. Housekeeping cleaned up the mess. And the landscapers and maintenance guys gutted and dressed him right up there behind the kitchen. [She pointed up the hill toward the hotel.]

"No!"

Yeah! Then guess what?

"What?!"

We had an employee party in the dining room—you know, beer, wine—the works. They had that guy's carcass on the spit out in the courtyard roasting. The cooks served him up barbecue style at the buffet table. We all had a taste—he was delicious.

Convincing and well delivered, this joke also functions as a cautionary tale and displays some elements of Gary Fine's definition of the contemporary legend: "A narrative that a teller presents to an audience in the context of their relationship. The text is an account of a happening in which the narrator or an immediate personal contact was not directly involved, and is presented as a proposition for belief; it is not always believed by speaker or audience, but it is presented as something that could have occurred and is told as if it happened" (1992, 2). As far as the audience is concerned, the teller appears to tell the joke only to her sister, a coworker, while the rest of us stand about. Of course, when telling this story of a "crime" she presumably can trust only a relative with the information. She is, in fact, loud enough and we're in a room small enough that we can't help but hear her. As in Fine's definition, the employee was not directly involved in the murder or preparation of the guest, but she does claim to have participated in the eating. And though not believed by speaker or audience, the story's details do suggest a certain plausibility. The story deliberately involves a variety of audience responses, which in this case were predictably mixed. The guests smiled politely, but by the way that they looked at each other, it was clear the joke had made them uncomfortable. The wranglers and employees of the lodge, on the other hand, burst out laughing. What surprised me most, however, was my own response. Though not a true insider, I joined in the laughter, with the added stimulus of my astonished disbelief that someone, even humorously, would express such aggressiveness toward outsiders. After having worked for a few weeks with Kit and experienced firsthand the rudeness of guests, I suppose I had more empathy than I had anticipated. For if nothing else, the joke serves as a warning to visitors that if they do not behave properly, their metaphorical consumption by the community will become literal. The joke's target is the stereotypic tourist—the impatient guest who complains about everything, legitimately or not. The narrator presents herself as one of the community of workers tired of serving silently those who can afford to stay at Sun Mountain Lodge. In this case, though, the guest's desired economic contribution to the community gets transformed violently into a total sacrifice, which allows the community to take everything it wants from the tourist and then flush it away.

As Walker explains, a joke like this can release tension even while admitting that the source of stress will not change:

> Humor is laughing at what you haven't got when you ought to have it. Of course, you laugh by proxy. You're really laughing at the other guy's lack, not your own. That's what makes it funny—the fact that you don't know you are laughing at yourself. Humor is when the joke is on you but hits the other fellow first—before it boomerangs. Humor is what you wish in your secret heart were not funny, but it is, and you must laugh. Humor is your own unconscious therapy. (1988, 101)

As many other critics have noted, humor can function as a socially sanctioned outlet for expressing prohibited subjects.[9] But when the we/they tension felt in any community gets heightened through economic dependence on a tourist trade, the sense of constant opposition never really weakens. In this particular story, the antagonism is expressed within the framework of cowboy culture—which, after all, is what the tourist purchases. Here we can recognize the paradigm of individuals' taking the law into their own hands but then having their crime celebrated as being committed for the community's benefit. The type of joking by a host community found in "Roasting the Guest" is marked by its suddenness and its swift disappearance—a flare-up. Certainly, this was the joke teller's own sense of the event. As the guests started getting saddled into their horses, I introduced myself to her and asked if she would be willing to put the joke on tape for my research project. "No way," she stated adamantly. She said that she would get in trouble if someone at the lodge found out she had told that joke.

The fact that humor of this kind is for many reasons an important tool of the horsewoman's trade is best explained by Kit McLean Cramer, when she responded to my request for a work-related humorous experience. She told me this anecdote at Sun Mountain Lodge, on a bench near the tack room, next to the corral. From there she can see potential riders hiking down a steep gravel path from the hotel.

LEAGUE OF THE LEGLESS

The only way to be in this job is with humor. People come down here to have a good time—now I'm talking about a majority, not every individual—there are exceptions for everything and reasons for being here that I'll never know—to please a wife or a partner—or something like that.

In a part of everybody, there's a small little corner in their heart that, I think, hangs on to the cowboy image and legend. I think it represents—I talk about this to other people—the cowboy image represents something that's very heroic and simple. And the more complicated lives get in Seattle, in computers, in the cities and all that kind of stuff, I think people look for that harder and when they go on vacation, for some reason a little corner of them is just hanging on to the cowboy dream, and I think that they come down here and part of the cowboy life is the camaraderie that they share with the people they're working with, which involves teasing and practical jokes and laughing.

You know, there's a good bunch of people that come down here that I just harass unmercifully. "Oh, my God, Kathy, we've got another woman here from the league of the legless!" And they [the tourists] think it's funny! I mean what an insulting thing to say—you've got no legs! I've never, I don't think I've ever irritated anybody by that. I hate to call it a smart-ass thing. I like to call it just teasing, in a way, and teasing in a fun way. If someone doesn't immediately grin, I instantly quit 'cause maybe it's not their thing. You've just got to feel your way around these people.

But God, those people I can tease and make them laugh, you know, I've got people whose horse's stumbling, kind of shakes them loose or something, and I say, "Now what are ya doin' with my good horse!" You know, I go pick on them. Really, you know, technically, I'm probably supposed to say, "Are you all right? Oh, geez, are you okay?" Instead, I kind of wade in and start picking on them. Course, I make sure they're okay—up and moving and not just laying there.

But ya know, humor's just gotta be here every day. (1995)

Within Kit's remarks on humor, tourists, and the American West lies a cohesive narrative with a beginning, middle, and end. She starts and finishes with the claim that humor is needed for her job. As in "Roasting the Guest," tourists in "League of the Legless" assume too much of the Winthrop community—servitude, entertainment, and acceptance. Unlike the cautionary tale "Roasting the Guest," however, "League of the Legless" does not advocate destroying or consuming the outsider nuisance. Here, the tourist's behavior is not inappropriate or unacceptable—only typical of a privileged outsider, searching for some nebulous friend. By greening the greenhorn, Kit remains within the conventions found in the western tall tale, but by expressing sympathy for the greenhorn and trying to understand the tourist's complicated emotional state, Kit adds to her narrative that common folkloric strategy of indirection. The greenhorn, a comic figure in the western community, is certainly here, but the excuses or explanation for the greenhorn's behavior lead the audience away from simple mockery or scapegoating.

In this way Kit also exposes how the tourist's cowboy dream is actually at odds with the Code of the West. Radner suggests that hedging of Kit's kind is a common strategy for "equivocating about or weakening" the message of the text (1993, 19). As in "Roasting the Guest," the tourist plays the role of victim in this story, but because of Kit's expression of empathy for the desperate, weakened mental and physical nature of the greenhorn, she is suggesting that despite its own western separateness, the community has a responsibility of sorts to maintain the fictions of the cowboy culture it values. Kit also allows for mixed motives within her target. Since she doesn't assume to know everything about the people who visit the Methow Valley, Kit can entertain the possibility that perhaps a visit might actually make someone else happy—hardly the stereotypic tourist's desire. Finally, Kit's own complicated status as a woman in cowboy culture not only makes her more self-conscious about the way she represents that culture to the tourist, but also allows her to appropriate a part of the cowboy dream while maintaining a gendered difference. Kit assumes the role of female hero in this western narrative, her own story.

Most important for this book, however, are Kit's remarks on how her humor mediates cowboy/tourist relations. On one level, joking and laughter are proof of the western dream: the tourist has acquired a cowboy or horsewoman for a friend. But on another level, the "league of the legless" teasing maintains a distance even as tourist and horsewoman share a laugh that doesn't necessarily imply friendship. A bit more explanation of the joke should be helpful here. More than one horsewoman impressed upon me the importance of leg length. If your legs are too long, the horse might buck; if they're too short, you will not be able to control the horse. Traditionally, such criteria for competence have formed part of the western code's trivializing of women, due to their supposed overall incompetence and physical limitations when attempting real cowboy labor. And yet there is an equally strong tradition of seeing such maladepts, whether females or tenderfoots, as harmless and even endearing parts of the larger social order. Cheree Carlson's observations are relevant:

> Comedy relies on the creation and castigation of a "clown" to alter consciousness of the social order. The clown is created not to serve as an enemy, as in tragedy, but as an example. The clown embodies all the problems of the social order, but even as s/he is separated from the herd, we recognize a "sense of fundamental kinship," a knowledge that everyone "contains [the clown] within." The clown is not an evil person, although s/he may do evil through ignorance. Comedy drives the clown away only temporarily, for the social distance we create in comedy is not to prepare the victim for sacrifice, but for dialogue. When the clown is punished, dialogue can begin, eventually leading to a rapprochement. Clown and society reemerge in a newly repaired social order. (1988, 312)

I see myself as a member of the league. As a stubby-legged woman, slipping on the gravel down the path to the corral, and as a relatively inexperienced horsewoman who needed her stirrups adjusted high on the stirrup strap, I soon had personal knowledge of how the clown functions in cowboy culture. During the time I was trying to learn more about horsewomen's work from Kit, she had me lead a group of tourist riders on a two-mile trail ride.

Like the other wranglers, I assumed the stoic and distant demeanor that distinguished me from the tourists. Kit was talking with a guest who was riding behind me. I overheard him asking why he had not seen me at the lodge before. Kit laughed and replied, "Oh, Kristin's my wranglerette." At the time I was thrilled that Kit considered me to be even that close to a wrangler. Now I can see I was more like a pet—or a clown. For example, I found out later that it is a comic tradition in the West to put the least experienced employee on an untried horse—presumably because of the entertainment it provides the real cowboys. For me that meant riding Buddy, the Butthead. In the arena Buddy loved turning circles and jumping over small barriers, but he was new to the trail-ride business and he hated it—balking and bucking, slipping and sliding down the hills.

And yet, instead of doing what would make both Buddy and me more comfortable, Kit made me ride Buddy not only during my lessons, but when I helped on trail rides. One day she told me to trot and gallop him up and down the dirt road twenty-five times. At ten o'clock in the morning, it was over ninety degrees. I had left my fishing hat at home, but Kit snickered at my new straw cowboy-looking hat. Sitting in the shade of her bench, Kit and another wrangler watched me practice, exchanging comments from time to time. My personal goal was to stay put in the saddle without grabbing the saddle horn. I controlled my fear of falling off Buddy during one of his moments of rebellion, and I was proud when, sweaty and dirty, I finally trotted back to the corral. Kit actually praised my galloping but reminded me to keep my hands calmer, closer to the saddle horn but not touching it. Then came the jab. "You kinda looked like one of those cartoon characters riding on a runaway horse with your hands flopping all over," she said, and suddenly this ludicrous image of myself filled my mind. Kit's remark put a new spin on my perception of successful horseback riding. I would need to do a lot more riding before I could possibly gain Kit's respect for my horsewomanship—and perhaps I really never could. While training Buddy and me, Kit and her peers found both of us amusing.

The tourist presents at least as good a source for laughter, but the transient and unexamined nature of the horsewoman's relationship to this visiting employer adds further considerations to the role of humor. In one sense tourists are objects of sympathy. As Kit sees it, these visitors, damaged by the complexities of city life and computers and further fractured by their desire for a "cowboy image," arrive looking for that western dream of "manly independence and rootlessness" that frees the tourist from responsibilities, from work and home (Lojek 1993, 189). As a result, for Kit and others the "league of the legless" represents a group of physically and presumably emotionally crippled people. In another sense, though, tourists represent all the threats inherent to the providers of services in an economy based on professional friendship. Tourists are economically well off, while the horsewoman's work is grueling, low paying, and seasonal, but part of this work is paradoxically to embody the institutionalized and romanticized fantasy of the cowboy lifestyle. Tourists pay for a companion in the image of the cowboy dream—someone who will teach them about life in the American West, make jokes with them, and spend a little time with them.

Given these circumstances, one possible explanation for Kit's humor could be simply that it is a form of veiled aggression—"a laughing chastisement for the tourist's insincerity, pomposity, stupidity" (Douglas 1975, 93). The "league of the legless" jibe, for instance, suggests that a large number of tourists, and in this case women, specifically share as a group a deformity from which Kit obviously does not suffer. A second operating force, and one I have already mentioned, is the humorous tradition in cowboy culture of needling the inexperienced rider as a form of general entertainment. The third and most intriguing function of Kit's humor, however, is as a coping mechanism for dealing with the stress arising from the responsibility of representing such intrinsic features of the American dream—the tourists' stress and Kit's own. Though Kit indicates that she would stop the teasing if the tourists/women obviously did not like it, she explicitly states that her "legless" targets "think it's funny!" The payoff comes when a customer is bucked off a horse—an incredibly unpleasant experience. Kit's female tourist was probably already intimidated by the idea of riding a horse, but because the teasing relationship is in place, Kit can use it to dissipate the guest's stress and fear after falling from the horse. Humor clears the air.

But in an important sense, the air can never be cleared. Because she works with tourists almost all day, every day, Kit is necessarily an excellent performer, and for a number of audiences. She carries out a challenging balancing act inside and outside the public and private realms of cowboy and contemporary culture. Economics demand such a performance. Though an authentic horseperson might stand apart and mock an outsider, a representation of friendliness is institutionally mandated by Kit's employer, who expects his employees to be experts in the field and to act professionally when talking to and riding with clientele. It is also mandated by Winthrop itself, which legally requires the cowboy/western motif on all structures and businesses. But Kit performs as well for an audience of her peers, Kathy and "other people" who also must conform to tourist expectations of performing the cowboy dream and who are also entertained by Kit's complex but enjoyable teasing of "the league of the legless."

And then there is me. As my analysis to this point should make clear, in Kit's story I see myself both as an audience and as the object of the joke—the tourist. With me as with her other audiences, Kit tells her stories well. She uses language with facility. She is quick and witty. She also has an amazing ability to repeat stories with little variation from one telling to the next—a sure sign that she tells the same ones frequently. And yet, although I am able to comprehend some additional aspects or narrative dimensions of Kit's explanation of humor on the job because of my personal relationship with her as a student and unpaid employee, and also because of my education in poetry and literature (which surprisingly often affords me other possible points of view on her narrative), a silence still hides at least some of her attitudes. As an outsider, I represent a technologically centered culture, which to Kit is unrealistic, confused, and decadent—so much so that its citizens value the imaginary rather than reality and come to Winthrop willing to pay for a friend who is an image. As a student of cowboy culture, I am thus included in the joke but excluded from it as well. The interview process itself sets me up as a stand-in for a variety of audiences, shifting positions in the narrative, except when Kit explains or justifies her words and behavior to me as the inquiring academic outsider.

Still, though much of Kit's behavior remains inaccessible to me, its general mediating force can, I think, be recognized. Except to me, her perceptions of her clientele as somehow pathetic are not revealed to outsiders. And yet her own awareness of that rigid, cowboy sociological structure, which demeans tourists and women, leads Kit to feel sympathy toward her guests. Thus, Kit's teasing makes fun of tourists, but also of the Code of the West within which she functions, especially as it relates to greening the greenhorn if newcomers are victimized either verbally or physically. To maintain her status as a serious participant in cowboy culture, Kit sustains the Code of the West by teasing the tourist. And yet her sympathy subverts it, for at times humor becomes a method for dispelling those tourist insecurities that arise from the tourist's inexperience and mistakes. Since this function actually smoothes over the tourist's rough edges that cowboy culture finds so funny, Kit's humor speaks to her own vulnerability, emotionally and economically, as a funny horsewoman.

And within this understanding, I recognize the privileged though alienated position I myself—part student, part tourist, part cowgirl—occupy as Kit's interviewer and audience.

CHAPTER FOUR

"NOTHING TO LOSE"

A Horsewoman and a Tall Tale

In many of the stories I collected from the Methow Valley horsewomen, I could not help but note a number of elements characteristic of the tall tale, even though my research had not uncovered many references to women in connection with that genre. The associations among humor, aggression, and unfeminine behavior may help to account for the scarcity of critical work on women's place within the tall-tale tradition, at least when compared to the richness of similar work on men. Discussion of western humor and tall tales, including those by scholars of women's humor such as Nancy Walker, still often implicitly or explicitly deny women that knowledge of the world that produces such stories and jokes.

When I first began mentioning my interest in humor and the western horsewoman in the Methow Valley, Shiril Cairns's name came up several times. Described as a hard-living, tough, funny, and articulate woman, for almost twenty years Shiril ran Rocking Horse Ranch in Mazama, Washington. She rented out camp spaces and trailer hookups, offered day rides and pack trips. She held children's day camps during the summer where they would decorate the horses, and she had taught part of an outdoorsman course in conjunction with a community college. For many summers she opened her home to teenagers with what she called "attitude" problems. For three to six weeks these kids worked with Shiril on her ranch. Later, during an interview, she laughingly told me, "Yeah, I let 'em sleep in. Then I go out and do their chores, and they get to do all the jobs no one wants to do—like cleaning out the chicken coop" (1992).

In 1992 I wrote to Shiril several times, explaining my project and requesting an interview. She did not respond. When I arrived in the area, I drove out to her ranch to ask for an interview in person. I parked near a small, neat but run-down house. A dog barked furiously as I got out of my car. Since there was no answer at the front door, I looked for Shiril behind the house, where the campsites were located. Near a small camp trailer, two men and a woman sat at a picnic table, smoking, drinking beer, and seemingly talking seriously. Putting on my "I aim to please" smile, I went up and asked if they knew where I could find Shiril Cairns. In a deep, suspicious voice, the muscular guy with long, dark hair and light moustache asked, "Who wants to know?" I was taken aback for a second. I had not expected someone to feel threatened by me, and I was also annoyed that this guy was talking for Shiril, who was obviously the blond woman sitting next to him. Still directing my voice to the blond, I explained who I was. Apologetically, the dark-haired guy again replied, "Well, sorry I didn't get back to you. I don't have time to write, running this ranch and all."

Now I was really confused and getting angry. Apparently this guy not only spoke for poor Shiril, but answered her mail as well. "Hey, I'm busy now," said the dark-haired guy in a friendly way. "Why don't you come back tomorrow midmorning and we can talk."

"But I want to talk to Shiril!" (I was almost blustering now.)

"I'm Shiril."

I did not believe her for a moment, and I know it showed. Shiril then introduced her friends as Carl and Edna. Fumbling with my appointment book, digging in my briefcase for a pen, trying to recover, I managed to blurt out, "Uh, great! What time would be good for you?"

"Oh, about ten in the morning would be good. Chores will be done. We've been busy, but not much is scheduled for tomorrow."

She turned and started talking to her friends again, dismissing me in a way that suggested she understood the depth of my confusion. Shamefaced, I slithered back to the car.

Shiril Cairns, 1990. Photograph courtesy of Meghan Sullivan

When I arrived a few minutes before ten the next morning, Shiril was well prepared. Coffee perked on the stove, and a box full of photos was ready for me to go through. Throughout our conversation, a cacophony of sounds filled the house—her daughters, Jessie and Meghan, her infant grandson, Steven, two teenage summer boarders, dogs, cats, chickens, and a phone that just kept ringing. Shiril let Jessie field most of the calls, but sometimes she would have to get up and answer herself.

We talked on two separate days. The first interview took three hours— Shiril had a lot to say about her life and work in the area. In 1992 she had lived in the Methow for fourteen years. Before starting the ranch, she did some wrangling, gave horseback rides, and worked for companies that packed people into the wilderness. Because she was outspoken and a relative newcomer to a place that treasures its pioneer heritage, Shiril was something of a marginalized figure, discounted by some community members. During this interview, she recalled how unwelcome male outfitters made her feel: "When I started getting into outfitting, threatening their territory, they resented it. They'd already pissed all over the wilderness. And by God, I better not get back in there. You know what I mean? They'd marked the territory" (1992). Shiril organized a Horsewoman's Association for women active in the horse business. They only met once, largely, Shiril believed, because the women's husbands and other male community members who worked professionally with horses felt insecure and discouraged their wives and girlfriends from attending again. In one irreverent anecdote, she commented:

> You know bull riding? Now, if that's not a male sport, I don't know what is. You know, I can understand why they [wranglers] had to buck out horses. You might need to buck out a horse. If there are a thousand horses running and you just had to pick up a likely one to gentle it, real fast—I can understand taking on that, bareback or saddle. I can even get the roping stuff. But you can't tell me that bull riding is anything more than a continuation of a "boys'" Sunday afternoon—too many beers and guys standing around saying, "I betcha can't ride Old One Horn over there."
>
> There is no purpose in the world to riding a bull—none at all. It's men, you know. One of 'em saying to another, "I'll betcha four beers I can stay on 'em for ten seconds." (1992)

At the end of the first interview, I asked Shiril to think of some scary stories and humorous tales for our next talk. The second interview took place outside her house. Under the shade of a large tree, I sat in a lawn chair and Shiril perched on the top of a picnic table. One of her scary tales focused on a mule that fell off the trail during a pack trip, careening forty feet down a hillside. Afraid that she might have to shoot the animal since it was not getting up, she took out her gun and hiked down. The mule whined and cried, and a patch of hide had been rubbed off its flank, but it was fine.

When I heard Shiril's funny stories, I couldn't believe how well suited they were to my research. All of the tales focused on the type of pack trip requested by guests, categorized as "standard" or "deluxe." Shiril preferred the standard trips.

A STANDARD TRIP

Seven women came to me—the youngest was thirty-three and the oldest was forty-six—seven ladies. They wanted to go on a pack trip because this was part of their husbands' rituals. But this was about two weeks before hunting season.

"Sure," I said, "I'll take you guys, but this is a 'standard' trip."

I'm loading up the pack boxes and there's one whole pack box of booze. "Hey," I said, "let's get something understood here. I'm here to take care of the animals and to get you in [to the wilderness] safely. As far as camp goes, and cooking—that's all up to you guys."

"Oh, yeah, yeah, yeah—we understand, we can do it," they said.

We get in there and I don't even have the packs off the horse before they're already trying to open the pack box to get to the booze. "Wait a minute here, guys," I said. "Why don't you get this other stuff and get your tents up?"

"Oh, no, no, no, we want to have a 'getting to camp' cocktail."

At about dusk that evening, I hear, "BETTY! I know you've got that pole upside down. I know you do!"

"What's this string for?"

"It's your tampon, you dipshit."

It was just going back and forth, [they were acting like this] because there had always been a Bill or a Mike or a Pete or a Ted to put the tents up for them. It was hysterical!

The next morning there was one tent that was half erected by a tree that had two ladies sleeping under it. Most of the ladies had the tents curled up around them. And there were two ladies still sleeping in the campfire—in the ashes of the campfire! (1992)

While I believe this pack trip occurred, Shiril had a knack at storytelling. As Lauralee Northcott told me, "Any story worth telling is worth embellishing" (2005). The next two stories definitely fit my research profile, but Shiril asked me to keep them quiet as she thought that some parts of the narratives might adversely affect her business in this conservative community. When I first wrote about the following stories, I utilized a pseudonym to protect her identity. Since Shiril died of cancer in 1998, I have had discussions with Meghan Sullivan and Jessie Dice, Shiril's daughters, regarding the stories. Both young women believe that telling Shiril's stories is a worthy endeavor. The stories defy typical expectations for women's storytelling and stretch the truth in predictable but unexpected ways in relationship to the tall tale.

The outfitting business is hard, demanding work. Shiril did a lot of the work alone in the wilderness while her daughters managed the ranch, giving trail rides, renting out campsites, and handling the countless chores on a ranch. As one of her humorous stories, Shiril began with the following:

ANOTHER DELUXE TRIP

Anyway, I had a group of five people for four days—*another* deluxe trip. I'm supposed to do all the stuff—packing, camp, cooking. So usually when you have a big group like this, you have a cook along, but the cook came down sick. So I had to do it all.

It was a good four hours after we'd gotten into camp before I got a break. You know, it's fairly hectic trying to get everybody off their horses properly and set your tack up so it's not going to be eaten by mice at night. Hang up all your blankets. All your saddles. All your other stuff. So I finally get all my stuff done and I sit down to have a cigarette.

I feel this hand on my shoulder. "You know," they said, "if you really understood Jesus you wouldn't need that cigarette."

I had packed in Seventh-Day Adventists without knowing about it. I had no idea! I knew that four days of this was going to drive me straight up a wall.

So, I got up in the middle of the night . . . at that time we were in a place where I had to use a hitch line, which means that the horses stay tied all night. I turned one of them loose. When I got up in the morning I said, "Ah, look at that! Billy's gone! I'll have to go find him!"

I took my cigarettes and my paperback book. I knew that Billy darn well would be down in the meadow about a mile below us, eating grass like crazy. I went to the meadow on a saddle horse and spent a nice afternoon, a nice day with Billy in the meadow. No people telling me "What about Jesus?" or anything like that.

I had to tie him [Billy] to a tree. When I came back at night, I told them, "Nope, I couldn't find him. Have to go out tomorrow."

I spent two days of this pack trip in this meadow having a great time. I don't know what they did.

The third night, I came in with the horse. They thought that I was just wonderful for finding a horse in the middle of the wilderness. They thought I was just—"Phew!" The next day we packed up and left. I got through it. (1992)

After hearing the next story, I decided that "Another Deluxe Trip" had been my audition. Since I had laughed heartily at her earnest guests, and since I seemed to approve of both her ingenuity in escaping and her desire to smoke, she went on to tell me the story I have entitled "Nothing to Lose." Had I reacted differently—less open, less amused, less tolerant—she probably would have stopped there, and for the same reasons that she had concerns about sharing this story with the community at large.

"Nothing to Lose" evokes many traditional notions of the tall tale, but because of stereotypic presumptions of women's behavior and status in the culture at large, the story's connection with that traditional form of narrative is diminished. A look at Jan Harold Brunvand's fairly representative definition of the tall tale can perhaps begin the process not only of rectifying this omission, but also of suggesting the consequences of such a revision. According to Brunvand, the setting of a tall tale often occurs in the wilderness or outdoors. The narrator tells the tale to a group of people—possibly peers, but frequently with a stranger present. Told to put someone, usually the stranger, off balance, the story confirms the narrator's status as the most knowledgeable and perhaps the most heroic person in the wilderness setting (1978, 136–37). James E. Caron suggests that often elements of violence, implied or explicit, are evident within a tall tale (1986, 27–37). Two factors apparent from these remarks would explain why Nancy Walker and others tend to exclude women from the tall-tale paradigms. First, women's virtual absence from the scenes and practices of wilderness expertise would make any claims to superior knowledge apparently unsupportable. Second, because women are socialized to be accommodating, not alienating—the perfect hostesses in a tourist town—the vigorous casting out of the stranger runs against type as well. Women are rarely depicted as physically or verbally violent.

As I examined the stories I had collected and scholarship on gender and the American West, women's apparent lack of participation in the telling of tall tales seemed to me to result more from gender than from ability. Within the realm of male and female storytelling, Farrer notes that "we have 'tall tales,' a male genre of storytelling; the female corollary is exaggeration. Men have 'stories' or 'yarns': women have 'gossip' or 'clothes lining'" (1975, xvi). When, for instance, Walker claims that women do not employ the tall-tale genre because of subject matter and place, is the problem that women are ignorant of the subject matter or place? Or that the subject matter and place are inappropriate? Or that women would be uncomfortable doing the necessary lying? Historically, women's absence as tellers of "lying tales" is certainly in keeping with those ideas about sex roles that pervade the American West and that also show clear signs of being cultural leftovers from certain nineteenth-century notions about women and men. While the western landscape may have made them more public and physical in their activities, nineteenth-century women were still represented as the civilizers, even though they rarely received recognition for their roles in forming or bettering their communities (Jameson 1987, 159). Though a case for excluding women from the tall-tale tradition might conceivably be based on any one of these qualities, male expertise and female decorum and honesty are employed most frequently.

Carolyn Brown writes that the earliest recording of tall tales came from people who met "tall-talking Americans" while traveling and that "early visitors to America, as well as those who never crossed the ocean but read the traveler's account or saw imported American plays, agreed that American humor was peculiarly exaggerative" (1987, 2–14). What seemed extreme or grotesque to others, however, could often be a weapon, a medicine, or a sign of membership in some community. Or as Mody Boatright puts it, the frontiersman tall-tale teller "lied in order to satirize his betters; he lied to cure others of the swell head; he lied in order to initiate the recruits to his way of life" (1949, 87). And this way of life, Walter Blair argues, may be our regional or even national identity, since American wit blends humor and horse sense together "to persuade or enlighten people of this country" in a way that appeals "to our love for homegrown laughter and our almost religious faith in mother wit" (1944, xi). Many of the women I interviewed claimed to have embellished their stories.

Barbara Welter explains that women's perceived task of maintaining a harmonious relationship between the sexes found its expression in what she calls the "Cult of True Womanhood" (1966, 4). Katherine Harris observes that by separating men and women into two spheres of influence, such a cluster of beliefs actually proves to be sociologically restrictive for both sexes:

> Women were to occupy themselves with the moral and practical issues relating to the nurturance of children and the management of the home. They were also to cultivate personal qualities of purity, piety, domesticity, and submissiveness to better meet the needs of husbands, fathers and children. Men, on the other hand, were to restrict their actions largely to the world of wage work and public affairs. They were expected to be aggressive and competitive, yet not too concerned with moral issues, for men were generally thought to possess spiritual natures intrinsically inferior to women's. (1987, 167)

If I apply this dichotomy to the realm of the tall tale, male spiritual "inferiority" would seem to provide a license for lying, whereas women would remain as nonparticipants, because intellectually, culturally, and morally such high spirits are "beneath" them. Mary Crawford claims "stereotypes about speech are central to gender stereotypes," with soft-spokenness linked to femininity, and assertiveness to masculinity (1992, 25). Such stereotypes have their effects even on self-proclaimed female liars. Vera Mark notes that women participating in the Moncrabeau Liars' Festival in Gascon, France, marked their difference from the male participants by modestly reproducing those "social conventions" that expressed "their ambivalence about performing at a male event while simultaneously representing positive images of women" (1993, 242).

Another explanation for the apparent absence of women from an occupational tall-tale tradition of the American West is the cultural implications and possibilities of a kind of systematic and formulaic gender behavior. Auerbach argues that "all true communities are knit together by their codes," which "can range from dogmas to a flexible, private and often semi-conscious set of beliefs" (1978, 8–9). Radner elaborates on this idea when she explains how coding within a community is not only multiple and multiform, but frequently exclusionary and even a subterfuge. She suggests, "coding occurs in the context of complex audiences in which some members may be competent and willing to decode the message, but others are not" (1993, 3). For women and their stories, this state of affairs is both repressive and empowering. Auerbach notes: "In literature at least, male communities tend to live by a code in its most explicit, formulated and inspirational sense" and, in the act of living, devote a great deal of energy to reinforcing this code as the culture's standard of meaning and value. In the face of such imposed authority, "in female communities, the code seems a fleeting thing, more a buried language than a rallying cry" (1978, 8–9). Radner says that the transmission and comprehension of a code in women's culture may be unrecognizable to the dominant culture.

Making a virtue of a hard necessity, Radner extends Auerbach's account by suggesting that within such a dynamic, only those who are excluded or subordinated can develop any real facility or versatility in their communications:

> Coding presumes an audience in which one group of receivers is "monocultural" and thus assumes that its own interpretation of messages is the only one possible, while the second group, living in two cultures, may recognize a double message—which requires recognizing that some form of coding has taken place. Coding, then, is the expression or transmission of messages potentially accessible to a (bicultural) community for whom those same messages are either inaccessible or inadmissible. (1993, 3)

Frequently, jokes or humorous tales reveal assumptions about gender and find their voice. Walker describes how humor often articulates not only the dominant, but also the buried codes of a community. As "one of the expressions of the codes within which a group functions," the "topics and forms of humor provide" an index to the values and taboos of the groups, and the humor can be so intimately tied to group identity as to be almost unintelligible to anyone outside the group (1988, 105–6). What complicates matters for the horsewomen in the Methow Valley, however, is that they occupy two subordinate positions—one in relation to males in their own community and another, which they share with these males, in relation to the tourist economy, the source of their livelihoods. As mentioned, tall tales put the outsider off balance in an unfamiliar environment, which West believes is a response to feelings of impotence and inferiority. Thanks to the economics of the situation, "the cowboy often had occasion to feel that tourists considered him to be an

object for gawking at, ordering around, and treating like a monkey in a cage."
Cowboys took their revenge by finding ways "to scare tourists into seventeen
kinds of fits" (1990, 50).

Yet, while the horsewomen's stories are often typical examples of cowboy
humor and the tall tale, as members of this community the women find
themselves occupying what Radner calls the "patriarchal designated feminine position" (1993, 4). Within western culture, when women are not keeping their mouths shut, they are assumed to use words primarily as a medium
for expressing emotion—a norm of discourse the dominant culture may
appreciate at times, but which it certainly does not respect. Consequently,
when a woman enters a professional realm that males consider their own,
she finds herself both included and excluded. Because she is more, she is
also less.

For the valley's horsewomen, cultural reality means that they must live
and work within a least two codes—male and female—and, regardless of how
they feel about it, they must constantly negotiate between these two realms.
Nor do they lack models or support in this task. The horsewomen I interviewed are but a few in this geographic area. They have a shared history. Far
from considering themselves the beneficiaries of some form of feminism or
affirmative action, they represent a tradition by promoting a viable cowboy culture. And by appropriating a typically male-dominated profession, the horsewomen have already to some degree opened up a critique of dominant occupational ideologies. To enter successfully into the language and occupations
of cowboy culture, however, even while reproducing them the horsewomen
must somehow subvert or rebel against the limitations that such convention
imposes. The recasting of cowboy language and varied spins on conventions
of the tall tale do not seem inconclusive or broken—briefly glimpsed openings or bursts of hidden culture, that "buried language" or "fleeting thing"
that Auerbach (1978) identifies as the female literary code. In fact, however
complex the internal dynamics may be, the stories these women told me
commonly end with a solid resolution—a well-tested secret, offered to me,
which reveals how the tellers learned to integrate, often through humor, their
professional, social, and personal lives.

The proof, however, lies in the telling.

Nothing to Lose

Well, I had this woman call me up and ask me about a pack trip. She said she and a friend wanted to pack into the wilderness for a couple of days. So I asked her for how long and asked her what kind of pack trip she wanted. You see, I offer two kinds of trips, the modified and the deluxe. I do the works. Not that I like it much, but we all got to earn a living. And it costs a lot more, you know, the deluxe. So, the woman said she wanted a deluxe trip, so we set up dates. She and her friend were from the west side [the Seattle area] somewhere.

Anyway, I met them at the trailhead a few weeks later. I got them settled on their horses and sent them on ahead. You see, it was just me and them. That's what I usually do if the customers can ride. So they rode up the trail while I packed up all the gear. It's a rough job getting all that gear on to the mules and I was just dying for a joint but I thought I better not, you know—the customers.

Well, later, I'm riding behind those gals, thinking about how nice it would be to have a toke, when I noticed something shiny on the trail. By God, it was a gun—a forty-five. I got off my horse, picked it up, and shoved it in my saddlebag. I couldn't help wondering why those gals would have a gun. I tell you, it made me worry. Now I really wanted to smoke it.

Later, I caught up to them on the trail and said, "Hey, one of you gals lose a gun?" One of them patted her hips.

"Yeah, I did," she said, taking the gun from me. "Sorry," she said.

I decided not to ask any questions, but I kept wondering about it. So, we finally got to the meadow where I camp my guests. The gals took off for a hike near the creek while I unpacked the mules and set up camp. I had to do every-thing—put up the tents, set up the kitchen, haul the wood, light the fire, and start the dinner. This took about two hours, and the whole time I'm figuring how I can get away and smoke a joint.

Just as I put the pot on for coffee, the gals come up from the creek dressed in their long johns, sporting gun-filled holsters on their hips. They're holding hands and kissing. Now I don't hold anything against lesbians. In fact, some-times I think it might be easier to be one.

So I say, "Hey, coffee's almost ready. Pull up a stump." So these gals sit down around the fire in their long johns. We get to talking about this and that. Finally, I ask, "What do you gals do for a living?"

One of them says, "Oh, we're police officers."

I've never been one to pass up an opportunity. So I put my feet up, pulled out a joint, and started smoking it right in front of them. Boy, that felt good smoking a joint right in front of a cop with nothing to lose.

I offered those gals some but they didn't want any. (1992)

Shiril's story seems to insist on its membership in the tall-tale genre—so much so, that a great deal of my laughter when first hearing this story arose from my joy at being given something so well suited to my research. The setting and props were certainly familiar. "Nothing to Lose" takes place in the wilderness. Except for the gender, the characters are tale figures of the American West—the female equivalents of cowboys and sheriffs, with all the accompanying ambiguity about who the outlaws might really be. There is even a mysterious gun, a forty-five, no less, which changes hands a couple of times and which certainly raises fears of violence in Shiril's mind. Both the narrative point of view and the story's structure follow tall-tale patterns. At first Shiril presents herself as a perplexed, somewhat naïve eyewitness. She sees a shiny object, discovers it is a gun, not surprisingly worries about what this might mean so far away from help, yet hands the weapon back over to its owner. Her surprised innocence is, however, at odds with her skill at presenting her narrative. She modulates her voice, and her face and body stress the key moments of tensions and suspense until her own exploding laughter signals the story's end. Certainly, Shiril Cairns could wield all the tools that Carolyn Brown identifies with "tall tale artistry," such as "the dead-pan pose, the variation in rhythm and timing, the sharp realistic detail, the absurd tall tale conceit, the comic understatement, the vivid naming" and "the skillful manipulation of the listener's values and beliefs" (1987, 28).

As for Shiril's narrative, both its central operating premise and its internal structure conform to widely recognized generic models. As Bauman explains: "Tall tales start out as apparently true narratives of personal experience, offered to be believed, with their ultimate effect traditionally derived by gradually bending the account out of shape—stretching the bounds of credibility bit by bit—until it finally reveals itself as a lie" (1986). Most critics agree with some version of this paradigm. Applying an analogy of height, J. Russell Reaver calls this pattern the "art of perpendicular lying." Tall tales begin with a "remarkable" but supposedly true event, "on top of which equally extraordinary events are piled." This "rising pillar of possibilities" has no limits but "the teller's fancy or his stock of traditional 'stretchers' or perhaps his audience's patience" (1972, 372). Even more schematically, Carolyn Brown suggests that tall tales are "constructed of three to five elements, three plot stages, with optional prologue and code" (1987, 20). Together, however, these elements enact "the comic contrast between the pretense of absolute, literal factuality and the outrageousness of the material," a contrast repeatedly invoked by the narrator's dallying "at the border between the credible and the incredible" (1987, 28), which, "like the metaphysical conceit of seventeenth century poets," links the subject "to something strikingly different" but which in the tall tale "creates the comparison comically, absurdly" (1987, 25).

I certainly believe that a kernel of truth lies at the center of Shiril's story. There seems to be no point at which she definitely slips over the border between the credible and the incredible. Largely because of my familiarity with the tall tale tradition, however, I am almost certain that in dramatizing the event, Shiril is not only piling strikingly incongruous images on to the "real" pack trip, but also organizing the events to best narrative effect. The story begins with Carolyn Brown's "optional prologue," in this case a rather rambling and mundane account of how a woman phoned Shiril to arrange a pack trip for herself and a friend. Along the way, Shiril describes the differences between a modified and a deluxe trip, complete with her own feelings about the work involved, but neglects to mention the sex of the woman's friend. Stage one of the plot begins with Shiril's admission that she wants to smoke a joint—a detail that for me in 1992 seemed very odd, since I assumed an outfitter responsible for people in the wilderness would want to keep clearheaded at all times. Stage two, the finding of the gun, follows immediately, a discovery that makes Shiril's earlier remark, "You see, it was just me and them," sound ominous and that joint even more desirable. Only now does Shiril mention in passing that her guests are "two gals," which makes the gun even more puzzling. But Shiril simply returns the gun, which one of the women takes matter-of-factly, and things go back to normal. The guests wander off on a hike while Shiril, still wanting that joint, goes to work.

After a two-hour interlude, stage three begins with a rapid series of sur-
prises. Wearing holsters over long johns (where did the rest of their clothes
go?) the women return, "holding hands and kissing." Suddenly Shiril's guests
have turned into gun-toting lesbian lovers, but she maintains her cool, just as
she did with the gun, and invites them over for coffee and a chat. The ensuing conversation reveals that things are even stranger: these women are also
police officers. In her life as well as her stories, Shiril had "never been one
to pass up an opportunity," and by lighting up her joint at last, now knowing
there is "nothing to lose," she not only delivers the punch line but leaves her
audience with a truly memorable image.

This moment also crystallizes that principle of comic inversion that commonly operates within the tall tale. As Ian Donaldson describes it, this principle involves "a sudden, comic switch of expected roles such as prisoner repri-
mands judge, child rebukes parent, wife rules husband, pupil instructs teacher,
master obeys servant" (1970, 5–6). In "Nothing to Lose," each of the narrative
episodes involves an inversion of this kind, concluding with the marijuana
smoker comfortably offering a joint to the police officer. Henri Bergson has
argued that this "topsyturvydom," so characteristic of comedy and maybe other
forms of humorous discourse as well, is a reaction against the idea of control,
of a closed system, of "the irreversibility of the order of phenomena, the perfect individuality of a perfectly self-contained system" (1956, 118). As Crawford
explains, it is this disruptive, overturning tendency that grants humor such
subversive potential: "Humor can be used to introduce and develop topics that
would be taboos in the serious mode, while protecting the speaker from the
serious consequences of having broken a taboo." But because joking offers "a
wonderful opportunity for a subordinate group," Crawford suggests that culturally, humor is "something that women cannot and must not do precisely
because of the subversive potential of women's humor" (1992, 36).

In her discussion of jokes, Douglas also argues that formally, the joke "con-
sists of a victorious tilting of freedom against control, it is an image of the lev-
eling of hierarchy, the triumph of intimacy over formality, of unofficial values
over official ones." In fact, Douglas goes so far as to explain her argument:

> My hypothesis is that a joke is seen and allowed when it offers a symbolic pat-
> tern of a social pattern occurring at the same time. The one social condition

necessary for a joke to be enjoyed is that the social group in which it is received should develop the formal characteristics of a "told" joke: that is, a dominant pattern of relations is challenged by another. If there is no joke in the social structure, no other joking can occur. (1975, 98)

Now on the face of it, pot-smoking female outfitters and lesbian police officers would at the very least suggest that "a dominant pattern of relations is challenged by another." But as I have tried to suggest, in this western community and elsewhere, the patterns of dominance and resistance are multiple and often contradictory.

With regard to audience, Shiril's story is complicated. If she were a male storyteller in the tall-tale tradition, she would probably be sharing this story not only with a stranger, but perhaps also with peers who had experienced similar events. But as I have already suggested, the storytelling tradition of women is not typically associated with public performance, which perhaps explains women's shadowy presence in literary accounts of the tall tale. The perception of who qualifies as a peer is another important issue. Is it other cowboys? Other horsewomen? Neither possibility is likely, since none of the horsewomen I initially spoke to in 1992 shared these types of stories. On the other hand, I am a safe bet as a listener. Though I own a cabin in the area, I do not live there year-round, and none of the horsewomen would regard me as an insider audience. Sharing stories with me does not necessarily mean sharing them with the community at large.

Patterns of dominance and resistance, as I have said, operate in Shiril's story. The most obvious subversion in the story arises from the common tall-tale motif of the insider's triumphing over the supposedly dominant outsider. As I discuss in chapter three, an analysis of who serves as the excluded or scapegoated figure in the stories throughout this book suggests some interesting modifications that could be made to narrative paradigms. Two targets tend to emerge. First and most predictably under the circumstances, since horsewomen's narratives necessarily encompass such themes as sexual harassment, identity, and mediation as well as variously gendered joking relationships in the American West, the resulting stories are often subversive belittlings of men. Though they are not expected to respond to the more reactive dimensions of cowboy culture, women's awareness of their unacknowledged but substantial contribution to the American West often leads them to assert their claims, which—within these dynamics at least—implicitly pushes men from their sole possession of the forefront. But another excluded figure forms within the horsewomen's stories, one produced not by gender or proximity, but by economics and the image of the American West itself. As individuals making a living in a tourist culture, it only makes sense that horsewomen would also use humor and the tall tale to set themselves apart, as experts, from the tourist. In fact, given a cultural environment that denies female ability, claims of authority made through humor and narrative would be more likely to come from women, whether they are addressing men in that environment or outsiders.

Regardless of their sexual orientation or occupation, the wealthy visitors in Shiril's tale pay her to work for them, and like any tall-tale narrator, Shiril inverts this relationship by showing how the outsiders are actually buffoons. The American West plays its part here, for in the wilderness the horsewoman takes charge, while the guests are incompetent and grotesque—losing guns on the trail, caught literally with their pants down. When Shiril lights up her joint and ends the narrative, she triumphs over her guests in a way that "reinforces 'performance' goals of competition, the establishment of hierarchical relationships, and self-aggrandizement"—a way, in short, that Crawford identifies with male humor (1992, 32). But as Kay Cothran notes, far from being restricted to this insider-outsider dynamic, the tall tale can also function as ammunition for disputes between the sexes and disputes regarding local issues (1974, 344). Despite all the gender distortions in this story, it is still crucially important that the teller and all the characters are female and that Shiril herself has an ambiguous, subordinate, and marginal status within the insider community, which claims superiority over the outsider.

In fact, Shiril's own history in this town could be summed up as consisting of disputes between the sexes regarding local issues. Though she worked professionally in a world that is dominantly male, much of the community judged her by highly prescriptive standards of femininity and found her lacking. Her work itself made her seem abnormal and threatening. In 1992 she was one of only three self-employed female outfitters. She was the only one who was single. Though a couple of old-timers did stand up for her, the male outfitters at first resented her. The state of the town's economy compounded this resistance. With few jobs available and low salaries as well, many people had two or three jobs just to keep living in the valley. As a recent arrival to the area, Shiril was therefore seen to be taking work away from men. In addition, such men often believed that women like Shiril (a single mother with two daughters) should not be in the wilderness at all but should be on welfare, taking care of her kids. Ironically, then, it was Shiril's self-reliance, her refusal to accept assistance, her solid western values that were often the cause of her clashes with "red-necked" authority figures (as she called them). As an example, there was one occasion when she was denied a Forest Service permit that would allow her to pack tourists into the wilderness. She appealed, attended a hearing, and won. But even Shiril admitted that it was "an extremely difficult thing for a woman to do, to face down ten guys sitting in cowboy hats and that are all treating me like 'little missy,' you know?" Especially in light of "Nothing to Lose," it is important to note that she felt this particular challenge was the result of a community rumor that she was gay. But in any case, her status as an outspoken, unmarried, recently arrived, job-stealing woman more than accounted for her "problem" with male community leaders. Of course, Shiril shares this position in relation to male authority with the female guests she packs into the wilderness.

Like Shiril, as policewomen these guests hold jobs traditionally held by men, and while this choice grants them some measure of freedom from traditional female role models, they no doubt often suffer the consequences at the hands of their police colleagues. Shiril, however, only learns about this parallel at the story's end. Before then, she is most aware of differences between them. Though all three are women, and Shiril even remarks that she sometimes thinks it would be easier to be a lesbian, she is a heterosexual insider and they are homosexual outsiders. What is truly remarkable about Shiril's story, however, is how it enlists the myth of the American West to create a space for all three women to free themselves for a time, in their own ways, from the felt weight of social oppression. As the setting for the story, the wilderness itself by definition lies outside the civilizing, restrictive influence of human society. It is also a place frequently inhabited by individuals who feel less stifled there—outlaws, outcasts, or loners. In this case both the narrator and the other characters appear as outsiders or rebels—Shiril, through her desire to smoke marijuana, and the other two women, through their open affection for each other. And yet for most of the story, Shiril is still constrained. Even after the guests openly display themselves as lovers, Shiril does not immediately light up. Why?

The answer lies once more in the tourist relationship and how it unfolds in the American West. Outsiders actually free themselves from restraint and the stresses and pressures at home by paying the packer to take on all the work and responsibility. Shiril makes a point of mentioning that her female guests have paid for the deluxe tour and also that she does not like doing all the work, "but we all got to earn a living." As with any working group, then, Shiril's job is to work hard and keep her mouth shut. Her guests count on this. They assume they can be open about their relationship because they have paid Shiril not to have an opinion, and she goes along with this assumption. Staying out of other people's lives and minding your own business are cardinal principles of both the Code of the West and workers in service industries. In fact, she manages to keep from asking the women about the gun even as she is handing it back—an incredible example of self-control, which contrasts sharply with the stereotype of the supposedly talkative western woman.

Everything changes, however, when the women reveal themselves to be police officers, which gives Shiril an opportunity she cannot pass up. What happens here is that Shiril recognizes for the first time the similarity between her guests' situation and her own. As Walker states, "the language of the text in women's humor reveals an awareness of discrimination and oppression at the same time that it wears a gloss of amusement" (1988, 45). Shiril's amusement arises from her awareness of the shared methods all three of them are using for dealing with discrimination. As a female packer, Shiril recognizes that she must seem almost more responsible, more professional than a man. As female police officers, her guests are if anything even more aware of appearances, since they are actually enforcing the laws of society. Shiril seems to suggest that illicit behavior is the shared method of choice for dealing with the stress. Her guests come to the wilderness because they can be openly gay there, without any fear that their supervisors will find out. Shiril's solution for stress is marijuana, but smoking it on the job publicly would be very unprofessional. The result is schematic. When Shiril lights the joint and even offers it to her guests, she silently proclaims: "We're in the same boat here. I won't tell anyone you're lesbians, even though you work in a profoundly masculine, homophobic profession, so long as you won't tell anyone I smoked some dope, even though professionally you uphold the laws which declare my action illegal."

In this way Shiril's story fulfills and revises the conventions of the tall tale. The story reflects the tourists' assumption that Shiril is a socially insignificant audience for their gay-life performance. The liberated guests still occupy a place of authority, until Shiril addresses them more personally. Though an element of the tall tale's one-upmanship drives the story—for Shiril certainly revels in the final act—she does not publicly humiliate them or represent them as total fools, partly because the effect of her last gesture depends on an awareness of how constricted and repressed the lives of all women working in male professions—or literary genres—can be. Her story therefore strikes a balance, reveals a shared knowledge, and negotiates a settlement between the narrator and her central characters. And this contract extends outward, binding her audience as well (though, I would argue, her presumed listeners are indisputably female). In her work on humor, Crawford has distinguished between men's conversation, which is preoccupied with "positive self-presentation," and women's conversation, whose primary goal is "intimacy." Given the discounting of women's value within society, Crawford argues that it would be natural for women "to be assigned the most trivial, low-status form of creativity, spontaneous conversational humor" (1992, 36). But in fact, because of humor's subversive potential, especially as a shared activity among women, Crawford notes that it is labeled an "unfeminine" activity. In "Nothing to Lose" the tension between the dynamics of humor, the community of women, and these specific women's awareness of their own strengths as successful workers in male professions makes any easy definition of a "woman's narrative" impossible. Though Shiril reaches a negotiated settlement of sorts with the police officers, the sense of one-upmanship still resonates strongly through the story—and beyond, because the circumstances of its telling produced a conclusion very much like the story's own.

Here my own status as Shiril's audience came into play. Like the women police officers, my initial relation to her was as a privileged outsider. A tourist

in the area, I was a stranger to Shiril. As an amateur in the wilderness, virtually ignorant of horses and the complexity of pack trips, at that point I was the
wealthy incompetent, and my association with a university English department and my graduate degree only made me more strange. It is not surprising, then, that she subtly checked out my attitudes and responses before she
told me "Nothing to Lose." We did, however, have some things in common.
Shiril was well read and liked to talk, which made one point of contact. We
were also mothers, with a similar faith in no-nonsense child rearing. And
finally, we had both been known to speak out on certain issues in male-
dominated environments and to receive negative responses to our candor.
Shiril also explored my attitude toward marijuana by finding out enough about
me to make a reasonable assumption. She was very interested in my age, my
background, and the year I graduated from high school. When she learned
that in the mid-seventies I had lived in a one-room cabin near Chicken, Alaska
(ninety miles from the nearest electrical outlet and flushing toilet), I think she
assumed that I was part of the counterculture of the late sixties and early
seventies and that I would probably not become morally indignant about her
smoking a joint.

The story that she shared with me did not make us equals; in fact, my
own appreciation arose from my awareness that though we were peers in
some areas, in others Shiril left me far behind. As a horsewoman, she was
a very impressive individual. (Getting off a horse on a trail and picking up
anything, let alone a gun, is actually no easy task.) I also found myself admir-
ing the depth of subversion in her tale. Even if I could be convinced that the
cops were as unconventional as Shiril considered them to be, I am not sure
I could actually smoke a joint in front of them. I envy at a safe distance the
bravery, the lawlessness, and the recklessness. And these qualities extend to
the telling itself. For, if nothing else, I hope this book has made clear that cultural norms about women's behavior endow their lying tales and jokes with a
potential for subversion that makes their telling often unsettling for both the
teller and the listener. As a result, like the negotiated silence between Shiril
and the police officers that ends "Nothing to Lose," her sharing of the story
with me was not only an act of generosity and solidarity, but also an act that

Meghan Sullivan (*left*) and Jessie Dice (*right*) heading back to the corral, 2005.
Photograph courtesy of Leslie Lanthorn

came with a warning and an injunction. Shiril was taking a chance, and she wanted me as a woman to recognize the size of the risk and to protect her from reprisals.

For as we all recognize, however different our circumstances may be, women engaged in traditionally male professions or in traditionally male narrative genres never have "Nothing to Lose." Shiril, the police officers, and I all work as females and outsiders on the fringes of cultural systems that reinforce stereotypic views of women and sexual orientation. Though Shiril's story allows for a certain degree of play, it must end with an uneasy agreement of anonymity and silence that binds teller, character, and listener. The story is packed with images of authority overthrown in a community and the larger world, which often find even the suggestion of subversion a cause for alarm.

Humorous tales can themselves be such suggestions, as Shiril's own negotiated settlement with me indicates. Shiril told me a story that contains not only a direct challenge to authority, but secrets that she did not wish to be shared with her community. I was held responsible to keep her identity hidden; further, I was also barred from having her story exactly as it was told.

EPILOGUE

Jumping Fences

As a researcher, cowgirl wanna-be, absentee homeowner, and tourist, I've learned a great deal about inclusion and exclusion while working on this project. Entering existing discourses extending from the culture of men to the culture of women, from the horsewomen and their tourist community to academics and the ideologies that structure and justify research, and from my girlhood wish to be a cowgirl to the place I have come to occupy as a woman conducting this project, has been physically, emotionally, and intellectually challenging. Making progress towards the horsewoman's code has at times been as exhilarating as riding over Horsehead Pass, and I've also been full of fear while riding next to an academic abyss that always seemed to threaten a wreck.

I have personally learned the truth of Radner's claim that "coding may allow women to communicate feminist messages to other women in their community; to refuse, subvert, or transform conventional expectations; to criticize male dominance in the face of male power. At the same time, because ambiguity is a necessary feature of every coded act, any instance of coding risks reinforcing the very ideology it is designed to critique" (1993, 23). In Winthrop, where maintaining the Code of the West is a matter of economic survival, even for unwomanly women this fact is lived as well as observed.

Similarly, seeking to liberate the horsewomen's narratives through academic discourse has led me to appreciate restraint and apparent silence as strategies, and not necessarily punishments, that can represent forms of communication and self-preservation.

In her essay "Deception in Search of the Truth," Jane Rule describes how her writing and research has taught her a great deal "about socially constructed expectations of gender, how little they really have to do with who people are, what they are capable of and what they need" (1990, 225). These remarks were especially helpful the time an acquaintance asked me when I was going to inform the horsewomen how oppressed their lives were. Apparently I was obliged to educate my informants, but I was taken aback. I felt protective—and then I had to laugh.

I have no intention of telling the women I have interviewed that they are oppressed. To begin with, they already believe I am an overeducated outsider and a prying wranglerette. I would not want to antagonize them further. And besides, compared to me, these women are emancipated. They make an independent living, working in difficult jobs while juggling the many domestic roles traditionally assigned to women. Without a hint of naïveté about practical gender politics, they do not whine or complain that life has dealt with them unfairly. Despite inevitable clashes from time to time, they work hard, play hard, and thrive in their community. They have also taught me to brush off the inconsequential, to make a choice and be responsible for it, to work for what I desire—and to keep a sense of humor.

Notes

INTRODUCTION | Cowgirls—Subversive Implications

1. As of June 2002, the Cowgirl Hall of Fame is located in Fort Worth, Texas.

2. The following books on women ranching and working in the West are slightly dated, but they provide an interesting sociological perspective: Katie Lee, *Ten Thousand Goddam Cattle: A History of the American Cowboy in Song, Story and Verse* (1976); Lynn Hanley, *Ride 'em Cowgirl* (1975); L. R. C. Macfarlane, *Eighty Years with Horses* (1973); and Alice Marriott, *Hell on Horses and Women* (1953).

3. Though tall tales can, of course, be told in a variety of settings, for obvious reasons I am emphasizing tales placed in wilderness settings. For an analysis of the genre's variety and diversity, see Carolyn Brown's *The Tall Tale in American Folklore and Literature* (1987), which provides an overview of such written tall-tale forms as the sketch, the anecdote, the hoax, and the frame tale (39–73). The importance of tourism in Winthrop and my own outsider status in the community make the dynamics of tall tales, shared between peers, secondary and frankly inaccessible in this study. I will note, however, that since many studies suggest that women would presumably have different speaking/joking communities than men, certain lying tales would be shared with only a few women—and certainly not always me. And in the community of Winthrop, the horsewomen I interviewed do not necessarily socialize together in any formal way. Lauralee Northcott, Marva Mountjoy, and Lynn Breaky-Clark are good friends, though. They have pajama parties once a month. "We call it the Bitch and Stitch Club," Marva said, laughing.

4. Kenneth Goldstein's *A Guide for Field Workers in Folklore* (1964) stresses scientific and empirical considerations. Anthony Seldon and Joanna Pappworth's *By Word of Mouth: "Elite" Oral History* (1983) proposes strategies for conducting interviews and provides useful material on the ethical and legal responsibilities of collecting oral history. "How to Do

Oral History," a publication of the Oral History Project: Social Science Research Institute at the University of Hawaiʻi at Manoa (1989) has also proved helpful.

5. Virginia calls herself a "cowboy poet," not a "cowgirl poet."

6. Meghan and her husband, Dave, recently closed Rocking Horse Ranch after twenty-six years in business. Meghan's mother, Shiril Cairns, started the ranch.

7. In the 1970s developers proposed a major downhill ski resort that never was manifested due to community dissent. Also, in 2000 a development company withdrew its fight to create a destination golf course in the same area after the community refused to support its efforts.

8. Recently, fishing in the rivers has been limited due to the imposition of EPA mandates regarding saving native salmon and trout species. Irrigation has also been restricted in an attempt to save the fish.

9. In the Methow Valley residents often refer to academics (Ph.D.s) as "posthole diggers."

ONE | Tourism, Gender, and Images of the American West

1. Many of Winthrop's pioneers were from Texas, which may explain the perpetuation of a Texan accent.

2. Virginia Bennett and Emele Clothier also played, often performing original songs.

3. A manny can be a rock or a piece of wood or canvas that blocks the water, creating a pool to pan in.

4. She is talking about herself. Marva does, in fact, refer to herself at this point.

5. A friend told me about a horsewoman who had been rounding up cattle all day—hard, dusty work. She came into Hank's Harvest Foods in Twisp, Washington, to order sandwiches at the deli bar. She wore a cowboy hat, long-sleeved cowboy shirt, jeans, leather chaps, boots, and spurs and was covered in dirt. Two bicyclers dressed in bright-colored Lycra bike shorts and shirts, wearing bike shoes, and holding their helmets stood with their mouths open, looking at the woman. One of them said, "That's a great costume. Where did you get it?" The horsewoman laughed and said, "I could ask you the same thing."

6. For descriptions of "greening the greenhorn" in cowboy culture, see John O. West, *Cowboy Folk Humor* (1990), 49–82; Stan Hoig, *The Humor of the American Cowboy* (1958), 145–59; Jo Rainbolt, *The Last Cowboy: Twilight Era of the Horseback Cowhand, 1900–1940* (1992), 151–65.

7. Kit McLean Cramer and Ella Black (Ella no longer lives in the Methow Valley) are the only horsewomen I interviewed with pioneer roots going back four generations in the Methow Valley. Three of the women I interviewed married into pioneer families.

Pioneer heritage is important for status in the Methow—it's what keeps the community exclusive, distinct from everybody who's outside that experience. Despite the fact that most of the horsewomen I interviewed have lived in the valley for twenty to thirty years, they would still be considered "marginal." Marva has more prestige, because she works for one of the most influential packers in the valley, who is from a pioneer family. But as a self-employed woman, Shiril Cairns always struggled for economic acceptance in this community (although she didn't care much whether people in the valley liked her or not). She was a kindhearted and innovative businesswoman. In the mid-1990s she cosponsored a community-college course focusing on the environment and the wilderness.

TWO | A Woman's Code of the West

1. Teresa Jordon, *Cowgirls: Women of the American West* (1984), 278; and Joyce Gibson Roach, *The Cowgirls* (1990), 1.

2. The perception of women as framed in a reduced heroic mode may also arise because the tales women tell are less classically "heroic" than tales told by men. See Carol Pearson and Katherine Pope, *The Female Hero in American and British Literature* (1981); and Barbara G. Walker, *The Women's Encyclopedia of Myths and Secrets* (1983). For the cowgirl hero, see Shelley Armitage, "Rawhide Heroines: The Evolution of the Cowgirl and the Myth of America," (1981), 166–81.

3. See Cathy Luchetti and Carol Orwell, *Women of the West* (1982), 14; Susan Armitage, *The Women's West* (1987), 13–14; and Jack Weston, *The Real American Cowboy* (1985), 167.

4. The riding dress for horsewomen changed from skirt to bloomers in the 1800s during the migration west. See Susan Brownmiller, *Femininity* (1984), for a discussion of the sociological, historical, and psychological factors involved in women's wearing pants (79–91). For an account of the cowgirl's costume, see Roach, *The Cowgirls*, 122–27; and Candace Savage, *Cowgirls* (1996), 36.

5. See Shelley Armitage, "Rawhide Heroines."

6. Shelley Armitage, "Rawhide Heroines," 166; Clyde A. Milner II, Carol A. O'Connor, and Martha A. Sandweiss, eds., *The Oxford History of the American West* (1994); Jane Tompkins, *West of Everything: The Inner Life of Westerns* (1993a); Weston, *The Real American Cowboy;* and West, *Cowboy Folk Humor.*

7. At Pard's Minimart in Winthrop, a large "End of the Line" painting adorns the wall behind the cashier. It depicts the owner of the shop dangling over the edge of an abyss. The town surrounding the gaping hole incorporates the names of local businesses that supported the establishment of the Minimart. The image reflects the dif-

ficulties the owner had in getting approval from the town of Winthrop for his store. According to the owner, several business owners were afraid that the Minimart would take business away from them and did not support the store and gas station. These businesses are conspicuously absent from the painting. Pard's Minimart burned down in 2005.

8. Kit McLean Cramer told me that as a child she used to pretend to be a packer by outfitting her two pet donkeys with gear.

9. The local Forest Service routinely maintains wilderness trails in the National Forest.

10. According to Kit McLean Cramer, the Harder mules belonged to someone with the last name Harder.

11. Kit was hauling out the deer that had been shot by the hunters as well as all their gear.

12. Kit used to work at Longacres Racetrack in Renton, Washington, as a pony girl, warming up the horses before races.

THREE | Tools of the Trade: Humor and Horse Sense

1. The helpful wife is a typical representation of women in cowboy culture in which ranch women, wearing flour sacks for dresses and untied lace-up shoes, are comic butts—foolish but helpful (Roach 1990, 193).

2. For the role of "play" in culture, see Roger Abrahams and Richard Bauman, "Ranges of Festival Behavior," in *Verbal Art as Performance* (1978), 193–208; Keith H. Basso, "Joking Imitations of Anglo-Americans: Interpretive Functions" (1979), 37–64; Don Handelman, "Play and Ritual: Complementary Frames of Metacommunication," (1977), 185–92; Francis Hearn, "Toward a Critical Theory of Play" (1976–77), 145–60; Jacob Levine, "Regression in Primitive Clowning," (1969), 167–78; and Jose E. Limon, "*Carne, Carnales,* and the Carnivalesque: Bahktinian *Batos,* Disorder and Narrative Discourses," (1989), 471–80.

3. For an outhouse, the packer digs a hole and sets a toilet seat on a stand over it. The toilet paper is put into a coffee can to keep it dry.

4. For an expanded explanation of this topic see Barbara Babcock, "The Story in the Story: Metanarration in Folk Narrative," (1978), 61–75. See also Charles Briggs, "Metadiscursive Practices and Scholarly Authority in Folkloristics" (1993), which explores the "meta" dimensions of text and textuality (387–434).

5. Joan Radner argues that women use self-reflectivity to trivialize themes in their narratives. See "Strategies of Coding in Women's Cultures" in Joan Newlon Radner, *Feminist Messages: Coding in Women's Folk Culture* (1993), 19–20.

6. Sam's Place was closed in 2000.

7. For a discussion of pards, see Shelley Armitage, "Rawhide Heroines," 166–81.

8. In 1994 I cowgirled for eight weeks with Kit McLean Cramer, head wrangler at Sun Mountain Lodge. I learned to ride English on a western saddle, to take tourists on trail rides, to wear a hat properly (and a proper hat), and to speak with a Texas twang. As a greenhorn to western culture, I also served as the butt of countless jokes.

9. In *Cowboy Hero: His Image in American History and Culture* (1979), William Savage explains the cowboy's popularity with prosperous outsiders as at least partially the result of identification: "he, more than any other historical or mythical figure from America's past, represents the fine middle-class virtue of common sense, and in action at that" (20). The functioning of the tourist's cowboy dream is a substantial issue to note. The important distinction here is that the tourist does not wish to become a cowboy, but rather to enact those parts that are attractive to the middle-class outsider. Those who vacation in Hawai'i no more want to become Hawaiians than visitors to Disneyland want to become Mickey Mouse. What is desired is the fantasy, not the assumption of identity. As a dream, the cowboy has become for Americans the essence of what is "best" in a certain vision of American culture. Nor is this identification with a fantasy cowboy culture confined to tourists. Cowboy postures are pervasive in American culture, as some claim individuality and freedom from authority but paradoxically insist that the larger community's institutions are illegal and un-American.

Bibliography

Abrahams, Roger D. 1975. "Folklore and Communication on St. Vincent." Pp. 287–300 in *Folklore: Performance and Communication,* ed. Dan Ben-Amos and Kenneth S. Goldstein. Paris: Mouton.

———. 1983. "Interpreting Folklore Ethnographically and Sociologically." Pp. 345–50 in *Handbook of American Folklore,* ed. Richard M. Dorson. Bloomington: Indiana University Press.

———. 1975. "Negotiating Respect: Patterns of Presentation Among Black Women." Pp. 58–80 in *Women and Folklore,* ed. Claire R. Farrer. Austin: University of Texas Press.

———. 1985. "Pragmatics and a Folklore of Experience." *Western Folklore* 44, no. 4 (October): 324–32.

———, and Richard Bauman. 1978. "Ranges of Festival Behavior." Pp. 193–208 in *The Reversible World: Symbolic Inversion in Art and Society,* ed. Barbara A. Babcock. Ithaca: Cornell University Press.

Adams, Ramon F. 1968. *The Cowboy and His Humor.* Austin: Encino.

———. 1969. *The Cowboy and His Code of Ethics.* Austin: Encino.

Aerni, Michael J. 1972. "Social Effects of Tourism." *Current Anthropology* 13, no. 2:162.

Alexander, Maxine, ed. 1984. *Speaking for Ourselves: Women of the South.* New York: Pantheon.

Allmendiger, Blake. 1992. *The Cowboy: Presentations of Labor in an American Work Culture.* New York: Oxford University Press.

Althusser, Louis, and Etienne Balibari. 1979. "Ideology and Ideological State Apparatuses." Pp. 127–86 in *Reading Capital,* trans. Ben Brewster. London: Verso; New York: Schocken Books.

Anderson, J. K. 1961. *Ancient Greek Horsemanship.* Berkeley and Los Angeles: University of California Press.

Apte, Mahadev L. 1985. *Humor and Laughter: An Anthropological Approach.* Ithaca: Cornell University Press.

Armitage, Shelley. 1981. "Rawhide Heroines: The Evolution of the Cowgirl and the Myth of America." Pp. 166–81 in *The American Self: Myth, Ideology, and Popular Culture,* ed. Sam Girgus. Albuquerque: University of New Mexico Press.

Armitage, Susan. 1987. "Introduction." *The Women's West,* ed. Susan Armitage. Norman: University of Oklahoma Press.

Auerbach, Nina. 1978. *Communities of Women: An Idea of Fiction.* Cambridge: Harvard University Press.

Babcock, Barbara. 1978. "The Story in the Story: Metanarration in Folk Narrative." Pp. 61–75 in *Verbal Art as Performance,* ed. Richard Bauman. Rowley: Newbury House.

———. 1993. "Feminisms/Pretexts: Fragments, Questions, and Reflections." *Anthropological Quarterly* 66, no. 2 (April): 59–66.

Bakhtin, Mikhail M. 1988. "Forms of Time and Chronotope in the Novel." Pp. 84–258 in *The Dialogic Imagination: Four Essays by M. M. Bakhtin,* ed. Michael Holquist, trans. Caryl Emerson and Michael Holquist. Austin: University of Texas Press.

Baldwin, Karen. 1985. "'Woof!' A Word on Women's Roles in Family Storytelling." Pp. 149–62 in *Women's Folklore, Women's Culture,* ed. Rosan A. Jordon. Philadephia: University of Pennsylvania Press.

Baron, Robert. 1993. "Multi-Paradigm Discipline, Inter-Disciplinary Field, Peering Through and Around the Interstices." *Western Folklore* 52 (April): 227–45.

Barr, Marleen. 1987. *Alien to Femininity: Speculative Fiction and Feminist Theory.* New York: Greenwood.

Barreca, Regina. 1991. *They Used to Call Me Snow White . . . But I Drifted.* New York: Viking.

———. 1992. *New Perspectives on Women and Comedy.* Philadelphia: Gordon and Breach.

Basso, Keith H. 1979. "Joking Imitations of Anglo-Americans: Interpretive Functions." Pp. 37–64 in *Portraits of 'The Whiteman': Linguistic Play and Cultural Symbols among the Western Apache.* Cambridge: Cambridge University Press.

Bateson, Gregory. 1972. "A Theory of Play and Fantasy." Pp. 177–93 in *Steps to an Ecology of Mind,* ed. Gregory Bateson. New York: Ballentine.

Bauman, Richard. 1978. *Verbal Art as Performance.* Rowley: Newbury House.

———. 1986. *Story, Performance and Event: Contextual Studies of Oral Narratives.* Cambridge: Cambridge University Press.

Bauman, Richard, and Joel Sherzer, eds. 1974. *Explorations in the Ethnography of Speaking.* London: Cambridge University Press.

Ben-Amos, Dan. 1969. "Analytical Categories and Ethnic Genres." *Genre* 2: 275–85.

———. 1971. "Toward a Definition of Folklore in Context." *Journal of American Folklore* 84:3–15.

Bennett, Virginia. 1993. *Legacy of the Land: Cowboy Poetry.* Bend, Ore.: Maverick.

———. 1994. "North Cascades Safaris—Gateway to the North Cascades." *Cascade Horseman* 7, no. 9 (March): 48–51.

———. 1997. *Canyon of the Forgotten.* Twisp, Wash.: Timberline Press.

———. 1999. Interview by author. Tape recording, Twisp, Wash., July 2.

———. 2000. Interview by author. Tape recording, Twisp, Wash., July 12.

Berger, Arthur A. 1987. "Humor: An Introduction." *American Behavioral Scientist* 30, no. 1 (January/February): 6–15.

Bergin, Billy. 2004. *Loyal to the Land: The Legendary Parker Ranch, 1750–1950.* Honolulu: University of Hawai'i Press.

Bergman, Brian. 2002. "Film: Cowgirl Feminism." *Maclean's Magazine,* July 22, 52.

Bergson, Henri. 1956. "Laughter." Pp. 61–190 in *Comedy,* ed. Wylie Sypher. New York: Doubleday.

Berlyne, D. E. 1969. "Laughter, Humor, and Play." Pp. 705–852 in *Handbook of Social Psychology,* vol. 3. 2d ed. Reading, Mass: Addison-Wesley.

Berman, Jaye. 1990. "Women's Humor." *Contemporary Literature* 31, no. 2 (Summer): 251–60.

Bernheimer, Charles. 1986. "Huysmans: Writing Against (Female) Nature." Pp. 373–86 in *The Female Body in Western Culture,* ed. Susan Rubin Suleiman. Cambridge: Harvard University Press.

Bindas, Kenneth J. 1996. "Cool Water, Rye Whiskey, and Cowboys: Images of the West in Country Music." Pp. 216–39 in *Wanted Dead or Alive: The American West in Popular Culture,* ed. Richard Aquila. Urbana and Chicago: University of Illinois Press.

Blair, Walter. 1944. *Tall Tale America.* New York: Coward-McCann.

Blanton, Owen. 1993. "Film and Videotape Review Essays." *Journal of America Folklore* 106:476–83.

Boatright, Mody. 1949. *Folk Laughter on the American Frontier.* New York: Macmillan.

———. 1964. "The American Rodeo." *The American Quarterly* 16:202.

Boorstin, Daniel J. 1961. *The Image: A Guide to Pseudo-Events in America.* New York: Harper & Row.

Boyce, Janet. 1999. Interview by author. Tape recording, Winthrop, Wash., July.

Breaky-Clark, Lynn. 2000. Interview by author. Tape recording, Twisp, Wash., July 17.

Briggs, Charles L. 1986. *Learning How to Ask: A Sociolinguistic Appraisal of the Role of the Interview in Social Science Research.* Cambridge: Cambridge University Press.

————. 1993. "Metadiscursive Practices and Scholarly Authority in Folkloristics." *Journal of American Folklore* 106, no. 422:387–434.

Brown, Carolyn S. 1987. *The Tall Tale in American Folklore and Literature*. Knoxville: University of Tennessee Press.

Brown, Dee. 1995. *The American West*. New York: Touchstone.

Brownmiller, Susan. 1984. *Femininity*. New York: Fawcett Columbine.

Bruere, Martha B., and Mary R. Beard. 1934. *Laughing Their Way: Women's Humor in America*. New York: MacMillan.

Brunvand, Jan Harold. 1978. *The Study of American Folklore*. New York: W. W. Norton.

Burbick, Joan. 2002. *Rodeo Queens and the American Dream*. New York: Public Affairs.

Butler, Anne M. 1994. "Selling the Popular Myth." Pp. 771–801 in *The Oxford History of the American West*, ed. Clyde A. Milner II et al. New York: Oxford University Press.

Butler, Judith. 1990. *Gender Trouble*. New York: Routledge.

Cairns, Shiril. 1992. Interviews by author. Tape recordings, Mazama, Wash., July 2 and 3.

Camitta, Miriam. 1990. "Gender and Method in Folklore Fieldwork." *Southern Folklore* 47, no. 1: 21–31.

Carlson, A. Cheree. 1988. "Limitations on the Comic Frame: Some Witty American Women of the Nineteenth Century." *Quarter Journal of Speech* 74:310–22.

Caron, James E. 1986. "The Violence and Language of Swapping Lies: Towards a Definition of the American Tall Tale." *American Humor* 5, no. 1 (Spring): 27–37.

Clark, Sally. 2002. *Cowgirls: Film Documentary*.

Cohen, Erik. 1984. "The Sociology of Tourism." *Annual Review of Sociology* 10:373–92.

Cohen, Sarah Blacher. 1978. "Introduction." Pp. 1–13 in *Comic Relief: Humor in Contemporary American Literature*, ed. Sarah Blacher Cohen. Detroit: Wayne State University Press.

Connelly, F. Michael, and D. Jean Clandinin. 1990. "Stories of Experience and Narrative Inquiry." *Educational Researcher* 10, no. 5:2–14.

Cothran, Kay L. 1974. "Talking Trash in the Okefenokee Swamp Rim, Georgia." *Journal of American Folklore* 87:340–56.

Cowan-Smith, Virginia, and Bonnie Domrose Stone. 1988. *Aloha Cowboy*. Honolulu: University of Hawai'i Press.

Crawford, Mary. 1992. "Just Kidding: Gender and Conversational Humor." Pp. 23–37 in *New Perspectives on Women and Comedy*, ed. Regina Barreca. Philadelphia: Gordon and Breach.

Cross, Paulette. 1973. "Jokes and Black Consciousness: A Collection of Interviews." In *Mother Wit from the Laughing Barrel: Readings in the Interpretation of Afro-American Folklore*, ed. Alan Dundes. Englewood Cliffs, N.J.: Prentice Hall.

Currie, Dawn H., and Valerie Raoul. 1992. "The Anatomy of Gender Dissecting Sexual Difference in the Body of Knowledge." Pp. 1–34 in *Anatomy of Gender: Women's Struggle for the Body,* ed. Dawn H. Currie and Valerie Raoul. Ottawa: Carleton University Press.

Dagnon, Bonnie. 1992. Interview by author. Tape recording, Winthrop, Wash., July.

Dary, David. 1989. *Cowboy Culture: A Sage of Five Centuries.* Lawrence: University Press of Kansas.

Davis, D. Diane. 2000. *Breaking Up at Totality: A Rhetoric of Laughter.* Carbondale and Edwardsville: South Illinois University Press.

Davis, Natalie Zemon. 1978. "Women on Top: Symbolic Sexual Inversion and Political Disorder in Early Modern Europe." Pp. 147–90 in *The Reversible World: Inversion in Art and Society,* ed. Barbara Babcock. Ithaca and London: Cornell University Press.

Day, Beth. 1955. *America's First Cowgirl.* New York: Julian Messner.

Dettmer, Elke. 1994. "Moving Toward Responsible Tourism: A Role for Folklore." Pp. 187–97 in *Putting Folklore to Use,* ed. Michael Owen Jones. Lexington: Kentucky University Press.

Devin-Smith, Betsy. 2000. Interview by author. Tape recording, Winthrop, Wash., July 17.

DeWeert, Terry. 1999. Interview by author. Tape recording, Mazama, Wash., July 1.

Dice, Jessie. 2000. Interview by author. Tape recording, Twisp, Wash., July 5.

———. 2005. Interview by author. Tape recording, Twisp, Wash., June 26.

Donaldson, Ian. 1970. *The World Upside Down: Comedy from Jonson to Fielding.* Oxford: Oxford University Press.

Dorson, Richard M. 1983. "Folktale Performers." Pp. 287–300 in *Handbook of American Folklore,* ed. Richard M. Dorson. Bloomington: Indiana University Press.

Douglas, Mary. 1975. *Implicit Meanings: Essays in Anthropology.* London: Routledge & Kegan Paul.

Dresner, Zita. 1985. "Sentiment and Humor: A Double-Pronged Attack on Women's Place in Nineteeth-Century America." *Studies in American Humor* 4, nos. 1–2 (Spring/Summer): 18–29.

———. 1988. "Women's Humor." *Humor in America: A Research Guide to Genres and Topics.* New York: Greenwood. 137–61.

Dundes, Alan. 1975. *Analytical Essays in Folklore.* Paris: Mouton.

———. 1987. *Cracking Jokes: Studies of Sick Humor Cycles and Stereotypes.* Berkeley: Ten Speed.

Etulain, Richard W. 1996. *Re-Imagining the Modern American West: A Century of Fiction, History, and Art.* Tucson: University of Arizona Press.

Farb, Peter. 1974. *Word Play: What Happens When People Talk.* New York: Knopf.

Farley, Ronnie. 1995. *Cowgirls: Contemporary Portraits of the American West.* New York: Thunder's Mouth Press.

Farrer, Claire R. 1975. "Introduction." Pp. vii–xvii in *Women and Folklore,* ed. Claire R. Farrer. Austin: University of Texas Press.

Fine, Gary A. 1992. *Manufacturing Tales: Sex and Money in Contemporary Legends.* Knoxville: University of Tennessee Press.

Fleischhauer, Carl. 1983. "Sound Recording and Still Photography in the Field." Pp. 384–90 in *Handbook of American Folklore,* ed. Richard M. Dorson. Bloomington: Indiana University Press.

Flood, Clair. 2000. *Cowgirls: Women of the Wild West.* Santa Fe: Zon International.

Freud, Sigmund. 1960. *Jokes and Their Relation to the Unconscious.* New York: Norton.

Gagnier, Regina. 1988. "Between Women: A Cross-Class Analysis of Status and Anarchic Humor." Pp. 24–48 in *Last Laughs: Perspectives on Women and Comedy,* ed. Regina Barreca. New York: Gordon and Breach.

Gilchriest, Gail. 1993. *The Cowgirl Companion.* New York: Hyperion.

Goldstein, Kenneth S. 1964. *A Guide for Field Workers in Folklore.* Hatboro, Pa.: Folklore Associates.

Gracie, Sally. 2002. "Welcome to Twisp: Valley Life." *The Methow Valley News,* June 19, B6.

Green, Archie. 1983. "Interpreting Folklore Ideology." Pp. 351–58 in *Handbook of American Folklore,* ed. Richard M. Dorson. Bloomington: Indiana University Press.

Green, Rayna. 1993. "'It's Okay Once You Get It Past the Teeth' and other Feminist Paradigms for Folklore Studies." Pp. 1–8 in *Feminist Theory and the Study of Folklore,* ed. Susan Tower Hollis, Linda Pershing, and M. Jane Young. Urbana: University of Illinois Press.

Handelman, Don. 1977. "Play and Ritual: Complementary Frames of Metacommunication." Pp. 185–92 in *It's a Funny Thing, Humor,* ed. A. J. Chapman and Hugh Foot. London: Peogamon.

Hanley, Lynn. 1975. *Ride 'em Cowgirl!* New York: C. P. Putnam's.

Harris, Katherine. 1987. "Homesteading in Northwestern Colorado, 1873–1920: Sex Roles and Women's Experience." Pp. 165–78 in *The Women's West,* ed. Susan Armitage and Elizabeth Jameson. Norman: University of Oklahoma Press.

Hearn, Francis. 1976–77. "Toward a Critical Theory of Play." *Telos* 30:145–60.

Henry, Ann. 1999. Interview by author. Tape recording, Twisp, Wash., July 2.

———. 2005. Interview by author. Tape recording, Winthrop, Wash. June 24.

Hogan, Linda. 1994. "The Other Voices." Pp. 80–81 in *Graining the Mare: The Poetry of Ranch Women,* ed. Teresa Jordan. Salt Lake City, Utah: Peregrine Smith.

Hoig, Stan. 1958. *The Humor of the American Cowboy.* Boise: Caxton.

"How to Do Oral History." 1989. Oral History Project, Social Science Research Institute. Honolulu: University of Hawai'i at Manoa.

"In Praise of Cowgirls." 1987. *Texas Monthly,* November, 110.

Jameson, Elizabeth. 1987. "Women as Workers, Women as Civilizers: True Womanhood in the American West." Pp. 145–65 in *The Women's West,* ed. Susan Armitage and Elizabeth Jameson. Norman: University of Oklahoma Press.

Johnson, Robbie Davis. 1973. "Folklore and Women: A Social Interactional Analysis of the Folklore of a Texas Madam. *Journal of American Folklore* 86:211–24.

Jordon, Teresa. 1984. *Cowgirls: Women of the American West.* Garden City: Anchor Books.

Kaufman, Gloria. 1991. "Introduction: Humor and Power." Pp. viii–xiii in *In Stitches: A Patchwork of Feminist Humor and Satire,* ed. Gloria Kaufman. Bloomington: Indiana University Press.

Kirshenblatt-Gimblett, Barbara. 1999. *Destination Culture: Tourism, Museums and Heritage.* Berkeley, Los Angeles, and London: University of California Press.

Kirshenblatt-Gimblett, Barbara, and Edward M. Bruner. 1993. "Tourism." Pp. 300–307 in *Folklore, Cultural Performances, and Popular Entertainments,* ed. Richard Bauman. Urbana: University of Illinois Press.

Kodish, Debra. 1993. "Absent Gender, Silent Encounter." Pp. 41–50 in *Feminist Theory and the Study of Folklore,* ed. Susan Tower Hollis, Linda Pershing, and M. Jane Young. Urbana: University of Illinois Press.

Kolodny, Annette. 1985. "Dancing Through the Minefield: Some Observations on the Theory Practice and Politics of Feminist Literary Criticism." Pp. 278–85 in *The New Feminist Criticism: Essays on Women, Literature and Theory,* ed. Elaine Showalter. New York: Pantheon.

LeCompte, Mary Lou. 1993. *Cowgirls of the Rodeo: Pioneer Professional Athletes.* Chicago: University of Illinois Press.

Lee, Katie. 1976. *Ten Thousand Goddam Cattle: A History of the American Cowboy in Song, Story and Verse.* Flagstaff: Northland Press.

Lerner, Gerda. 1993. *The Creation of Feminist Consciousness: From the Middle Ages to Eighteen Seventy.* London: Oxford University Press.

Levine, Jacob. 1969. "Regression in Primitive Clowning." Pp. 167–78 in *Motivation in Humor.* New York: Atherton.

Limon, Jose E. 1989. "*Carne, Carnales,* and the Carnivalesque: Bakhtinian *Batos,* Disorder, and Narrative Discourses." *American Ethnologist* 16, no. 3:471–80.

Little, Judy. 1983. *Comedy and the Woman Writer.* Lincoln and London: University of Nebraska Press.

———. 1991. "Humoring the Sentence: Women's Dialogic Comedy." Pp. 19–31 in *Women's Comic Visions,* ed. June Sochen. Detroit: Wayne State University Press.

Lojeck, Helen. 1993. "Reading the Myth of the West." Pp. 184–97 in *Old West—New West: Centennial Essays*, ed. Barbara H. Meldrum. Moscow: University of Idaho Press.

Luchetti, Cathy, and Carol Olwell. 1982. *Women of the West*. New York: Orion Books.

MacCannell, Dean. 1976. *The Tourist: A New Theory of the Leisure Class*. New York: Schocken.

Macfarlane, L. R. C. 1973. *Eighty Years with Horses*. Wellington: Reed.

Mally-Burkhart, Judy. 1992. Interview by author. Tape recording, Mazama, Wash., July 3.

———. 2000. Interview by author. Tape recording, Mazama, Wash., July 18.

———. 2002. Interview by author. Tape recording, Mazama, Wash., July.

———. 2003. Interview by author. Telephone. March.

Marcus, Jane. 1988. "Daughters of Anger/Material Girls: Con/Textualizing Feminist Criticism." Pp. 281–307 in *Last Laughs: Perspectives on Women and Comedy*, ed. Regina Barreca. New York: Gordon and Breach.

Mark, Vera. 1993. "Peasant Grandmother, Hunting Helpmate, Silent Wife: Women and Text in Gascon Tall Tales." Pp. 238–51 in *Feminist Theory and the Study of Folklore*, ed. Susan Tower Hollis, Linda Pershing, and M. Jane Young. Urbana: University of Illinois Press.

Marks, Elaine, and Isabelle de Courtivron, eds. 1980. *New French Feminisms: An Anthology*. Amherst: University of Massachusetts Press.

Marriott, Alice. 1953. *Hell on Horses and Women*. Norman: University of Oklahoma Press.

Marvine, Dee. 1987. "Fannie Sperry Wowed 'em at the First Calgary Stampede." *American West*, August, 30–37.

McAndrews, Kristin M. 1999. "A Horsewoman and a Tall Tale." Pp. 63–73 in *Folklore*, vol. 110, ed. Gillian Bennett. London: Folklore Society.

McCarl, Robert. 1986. "Occupational Folklore." Pp. 71–88 in *Folk Groups and Folklore Genres: An Introduction*, ed. Elliot Oring. Logan: Utah State University Press.

McGinnis, Vera. 1974. *Rodeo Road; My Life as a Pioneer Cowgirl*. New York: Hastings House.

McLean Cramer, Kit. 1995. Interview by author. Tape recording, Twisp, Wash., July.

McNamara, Mary. 1992. "Laughing All the Way to the Revolution: The New Feminist Comics." *MS.*, January/February, 23–27.

Mills, Margaret. 1990. "Critical Theory and the Folklorists: Performance Interpretive Authority, and Gender." *Southern Folklore* 47, no. 1:5–15.

Milner II, Clyde A., Carol A. O'Connor, and Martha A. Sandweiss, eds. 1994. *The Oxford History of the American West*. New York: Oxford University Press.

Mindess, Harvey. 1987. "The Panorama of Humor and the Meaning of Life." *American Behavioral Scientist* 30, no. 1:82–95.

Minister, Kristina. 1991. "A Feminist Frame for the Oral History Interview." Pp. 27–41 in *Women's Works: The Feminist Practice of Oral History,* ed. Sherna Berger Gluck and Daphne Patai. New York and London: Routledge.

Mitchell, Carol. 1977. "The Sexual Perspective in the Appreciation and Interpretation of Jokes." *Western Folklore* 36:303–29.

———. 1985. "Some Differences in Male and Female Joke-Telling." Pp. 163–86 in *Women's Folklore, Women's Culture,* ed. Rosan A. Jordon. Philadelphia: University of Pennsylvania Press.

———. 1993. "Feminist Lenses and Female Folklore." Pp. 277–84 in *Feminist Theory and the Study of Folklore,* ed. Susan Tower Hollis, Linda Pershing, and M. Jane Young. Urbana: University of Illinois Press.

Mitchell, Roger. 1983. "Occupational Folklore: The Outdoor Industries." Pp. 128–35 in *Handbook of American Folklore,* ed. Richard M. Dorson. Bloomington: Indiana University Press.

Montgomery, Babe. 1994. Interview by author. Tape recording, Twisp, Wash., July 1 and 2.

Mountjoy, Marva. 1995. Interview by author. Tape recording, Winthrop, Wash., July 20.

———. 1996. Interview by author. July 17.

———. 2000. Interview by author. June 27.

Myres, Sandra L. 1982. *Westering Women and the Frontier Experience: 1800–1915.* Albuquerque: University of New Mexico Press.

Nenola, Aili. 1993. "Folklore and the Genderized World: Or Twelve Points from a Feminist Perspective." Pp. 49–61 in *Nordic Frontiers: Recent Issues in the Study of Modern Traditional Culture in the Nordic Countries,* ed. Pertti J. Anttonen and Reimund Kvideland. Turku: Nordic Institute of Folklore.

Northcott, Lauralee. 1999. Interview by author. Tape recording, Winthrop, Wash., July 21.

———. 2003. *Car Tunes.* Compact disc. March.

———. 2003. Interview by author. Telephone, March 23.

———. 2005. Interview by author. Tape recording, Winthrop, Wash., June 24.

Nuñez, Theron. 1989. "Tourist Studies in Anthropological Perspective." Pp. 265–79 in *Hosts and Guests: The Anthropology of Tourism,* ed. Valene L. Smith. Philadephia: University of Pennsylvania Press.

Oring, Elliott. 1992. *Jokes and Their Relations.* Lexington: University of Kentucky Press.

Pearson, Carol, and Katherine Pope. 1981. *The Female Hero in American and British Literature.* New York: Bowker.

Pershing, Linda. 1991. "There's a Joker in the Menstrual Hut: A Performance Analysis of Comedian Kate Clinton." Pp. 193–236 in *Women's Comic Visions*, ed. June Sochen. Detroit: Wayne State University Press.

Pinkster, Sanford. 1978. "The Urban Tall Tale: Frontier Humor in a Contemporary Key." Pp. 249–62 in *Comic Relief: Humor in Contemporary American Literature*, ed. Sarah Blacher Cohen. Detroit: Wayne State University Press.

Portman, Sally. 1993. *The Smiling Country.* Winthrop, Wash.: Sun Mountain Resorts.

Radner, Joan Newlon, ed. 1993. *Feminist Messages: Coding in Women's Folk Culture.* Urbana and Chicago: University of Illinois Press.

Rainbolt, Jo. 1992. *The Last Cowboy: Twilight Era of the Horseback Cowhand, 1900–1940.* Helena, Mont.: American and World Geographic.

Reaver, J. Russell. 1972. "From Reality to Fantasy: Opening-Closing Formulas in the Structures of American Tall Tales." *Southern Folklore Quarterly* 36 (December): 369–81.

Redden, Paul. 1999. *Wild West Shows.* Urbana and Chicago: University of Illinois Press.

Riley, Glenda. 1988. *The Female Frontier: A Comparative View of Women on the Prairie and the Plains.* Kansas: University Press of Kansas.

Riske, Milt. 1983. *Those Magnificent Cowgirls.* Cheyenne: Wyoming Publishing.

Roach, Joyce Gibson. 1990. *The Cowgirls.* Denton: University of North Texas Press.

Rothman, Hal. 1998. *Devil's Bargains: Tourism in the Twentieth-Century American West.* Lawrence: University Press of Kansas.

Rourke, Constance. 1931. *American Humor: A Study of the National Character.* Garden City: Doubleday.

Rowe, Kathleen. 1995. *The Unruly Woman: Gender and the Genres of Laughter.* Austin: University of Texas Press.

Rule, Jane. 1990. "Deception in Search of the Truth." Pp. 225–28 in *Language in Her Eye: Writing and Gender*, ed. Libby Scheier, Sara Sheard, and Eleanor Wachtel. Toronto: Coach House.

Russell, Don. 1970. *The Wild West.* Fort Worth: Amon Carter Museum of Western Art.

Russo, Mary. 1986. "Female Grotesques: Carnival and Theory." Pp. 213–29 in *Feminist Studies: Critical Studies*, ed. Teresa de Laurentis. Bloomington: Indiana University Press.

Saltzman, Rachelle H. 1993. "A Feminist Folklorist Encounters the Folk: Can Praxis Make Perfect?" Pp. 51–70 in *Feminist Theory and the Study of Folklore*, ed. Susan Tower Hollis, Linda Pershing, and M. Jane Young. Urbana: University of Illinois Press. 51–70.

Savage, Candace. 1996. *Cowgirls.* Vancouver and Toronto: Greystone.

Savage, Jr., William W. 1979. *The Cowboy Hero: His Image in American History and Culture.* Norman: University of Oklahoma Press.

Seagraves, Anne. 1991. *Women Who Charmed the West.* Hayden, Idaho: Wesanne.

———. 1992. *High-Spirited Women of the West.* Hayden, Idaho: Wesanne.

Seldon, Anthony, and Joanna Pappworth. 1983. *By Word of Mouth: "Elite" Oral History.* London and New York: Methuen.

Sheppard, Alice. 1991. "Social Cognition, Gender Roles, and Women's Humor." Pp. 33–56 in *Women's Comic Visions,* ed. June Sochen. Detroit: Wayne State University Press.

Shuman, Amy. 1993. "Dismantling Local Culture." *Western Folklore* 52 (April, July, October): 345–64.

Simon, Richard Keller. 1985. *The Labyrinth of the Comic: Theory and Practice from Fielding to Freud.* Tallahassee: Florida University Press.

Slotkin, Richard. 1973. *Regeneration Through Violence: Mythology of the American Frontier, 1600–1860.* Hanover, N.H.: Wesleyan University Press.

Smith, Valene. 1989. *Hosts and Guests: The Anthropology of Tourism.* Philadelphia: University of Pennsylvania Press.

Spiwak, Bob. 2003. "Not Just Horsing Around: Animals and People Coexist Happily on an Unusual Ranch." *Okanogan: Ruralite* (March): 4–5.

Stacey, Judith. 1991. "Can There Be a Feminist Ethnography?" Pp. 111–19 in *Women's Words: The Feminist Practice of Oral History,* ed. Sherna B. Gluck and Daphne Patai. New York: Routledge.

Stern, Stephen. 1991. "The Influence of Diversity on Folklore Studies in the Decades of the 1980's and '90's." *Western Folklore* 50 (January): 21–27.

Stoecklein, David R. 1999. *Cowgirls: Commemorating the Women of the West.* Ketchum, Idaho: David R. Stoecklein Photography and Publishing.

Stoeltje, Beverly J. 1975. "'A Helpmate for Man Indeed': The Image of the Frontier Woman." Pp. 25–41 in *Women and Folklore,* ed. Claire Farrer. Austin: University of Texas Press.

Sullivan, Meghan. 1999. Interview by author. Tape recording, Twisp, Wash., July.

———. 2000. Interview by author. Tape recording, Twisp, Wash., July.

Tompkins, Jane. 1993a. *West of Everything: The Inner Life of Westerns.* New York: Oxford University Press.

———. 1993b. "Women and the Language of Men." Pp. 43–59 in *Old West—New West: Centennial Essays,* ed. Barbara H. Meldrum. Moscow: University of Idaho Press.

Toth, Emily. 1984. "A Laughter of Their Own: Women's Humor in the United States." Pp. 199–215 in *Critical Essays on American Humor,* ed. William Bedford Clark and W. Craig Turner. Boston: C. K. Hall.

Van Cleve, Barbara. 1995. *Hard Twist: Western Ranch Women*. Santa Fe: Museum of New Mexico Press.

Walker, Barbara G. 1983. *The Woman's Encyclopedia of Myths and Secrets*. San Francisco: Harper and Row.

Walker, Nancy A. 1985. "Humor and Gender Roles: The 'Funny' Feminism of the Post–World War II Suburbs." *American Quarterly* 37:98–113.

———. 1988. *A Very Serious Thing: Women's Humor and American Culture*. Minneapolis: University of Minnesota Press.

———. 1991. "Toward Solidarity: Women's Humor and Group Identity." Pp. 57–81 in *Women's Comic Visions*, ed. June Sochen. Detroit: Wayne State University Press.

———, and Zita Dresner, eds. 1999. *Redressing the Balance: American Women's Literary Humor from Colonial Times to the 1980's*. Jackson: University Press of Mississippi.

Wallis, Sue. 1999. "Spirit of the Cowgirl." Pp. 17–22 in *Cowgirls: Commemorating the Women of the West*, ed. David R. Stoecklein. Ketchum, Idaho: David R. Stoecklein Photography and Publishing.

Welter, Barbara. 1966. "The Culture of True Womanhood, 1829–1860." *American Quarterly* 18 (Summer): 151–74.

West, John O. 1990. *Cowboy Folk Humor: Life and Laughter in the American West*. Little Rock: August House.

Weston, Jack. 1985. *The Real American Cowboy*. New York: Schocken.

Whatley, Mariamne H., and Elissa R. Henken. 2000. *Did You Hear about the Girl Who . . . ?: Contemporary Legends, Folklore and Human Sexuality*. New York and London: New York University Press.

Wister, Owen. 1902. *The Virginian: A Horseman of the Plains*. New York: Macmillan.

Workman, Mark. 1992. "Narratable and Unnarratable Lives." *Western Folklore* 51 (January): 97–107.

Yocum, Margaret R. 1985. "Woman to Woman: Fieldwork and the Private Sphere." Pp. 45–53 in *Women's Folklore, Women's Culture*, ed. Rosan A. Jordon. Philadephia: University of Pennsylvania Press.

———. 1990. "Fieldwork, Gender, and Transformation: The Second Way of Knowing." *Southern Folklore* 47, no. 1:33–44.

Young, M. Jane, and Kay Turner. 1993. "Challenging the Canon: Folklore Theory Reconsidered from Feminist Perspectives." Pp. 9–28 in *Feminist Theory and the Study of Folklore*, ed. Susan Tower Hollis, Linda Pershing, and M. Jane Young. Urbana and Chicago: University of Illinois Press.

Biographies

Now living east of Paso Robles, California, VIRGINIA BENNETT and her husband, Pete, manage the Bonel Ranch. She has been featured at the National Cowboy Poetry Gathering and on PBS and National Public Radio specials. Virginia is the author of *Legacy of the Land, Canyon of the Forgotten,* and *In the Company of Horses,* and her work has appeared in numerous anthologies. She is the editor of *Cowgirl Poetry: 100 years of Ridin' and Rhymin'* and *Cowboy Poetry: The Reunion.*

LYNN BREAKY-CLARK teaches half-time at the Alternative School in Twisp, Washington. In the summer she packs into the wilderness with a variety of outfitters. She regularly works for Miller-Blue Outfitting as a wagon driver, and during the winter she cooks for sleigh rides at Sun Mountain Lodge. Lynn likes the flexibility of her jobs. "If it's not fun," she says, "I'm not gonna do it."

In January 1998 SHIRIL CAIRNS died of liver cancer. She was forty-nine years old. Shiril had little experience with horses when she moved to the Methow Valley, but she learned on the job. When my mother, Patricia, told her that she didn't ride because horses didn't like her, Shiril said dryly, "Hey, honey, they don't like me either. I still ride." Shiril's summer art program was popular with children, as they were allowed to finger paint the horses. She raised two talented daughters, Meghan Sullivan and Jessie Dice, on the ranch. In 2004 Rocking Horse Ranch closed after twenty-six years in business.

A busy veterinarian in Winthrop, Washington, BETSY DEVIN-SMITH has branched out. Recently, she and her family sold most of the family's cattle herd. Betsy's love for cattle is now partially satisfied by Sue, a Jersey milk cow, and Mabel, a calf. "I call Sue a ski cow because when the snow flies I dry her up and so I can quit milking," she said. Betsy grazes about 150 head of hungry sheep throughout the upper Methow Valley. She has found a niche market in wool blankets and lamb.

TERRY DEWEERT has a brisk veterinary and horse-breeding business in Twisp, Washington. She took her Paint horse, Dina, to the Paint World Shows in 2003 and placed sixth in amateur honors. Dina has also won a number of other horse competitions. Behind her clinic, Terry built a one-hundred-foot-diameter pen for cow-cutting practice and uses buffalo instead of cows. "Four of us," she said, "work our cow cutters on the buffies." She also performs embryo transfers from show mares to recipient mares (treated with hormones), which allows her to keep presenting the show mares at competitions.

JESSIE DICE moved back to the Methow Valley about six months ago. Currently, she works for Betsy Devin-Smith and keeps her horses down the road from her house. She lives about a mile and a half from her sister, MEGHAN SULLIVAN. Jessie wants to make some money, ride when she can, and see "what life throws at me."

ANN HENRY retired as a pack cook a few years ago. These days she hikes and visits with her family. Her schedule is her own, and "I do what pleases me," she says. She is on the board of Room One, the Methow Conservancy, and the Methow Valley Education Foundation. Ann volunteers at the Confluence Gallery in Twisp, Washington. When she is not working on Washington trail maintenance, she also volunteers once a week at the Cove, a nonprofit organization that helps low-income families.

KIT MCLEAN CRAMER still works full-time for Claude Miller running cows and horses but mostly wrangling at the horse concession at Sun Mountain Lodge. KELSEY GRAY, her daughter, is now fourteen years old and in middle school. Five years ago Kit married Hank Cramer, a folk singer, in Shafer Meadow at Sun Mountain Lodge, where they met. Since I first interviewed her in 1995, Kit has remodeled one house and built another. She has also started Kit's Livery and Stables, where she boards horses. For the past year she has volunteered at the Shafer Museum, doing computer archiving of turn-of-the-century and pioneer photographs from Methow Valley residents. With Hank and Kelsey, she has been enjoying traveling.

JUDY MALLY-BURKHART takes pleasure in riding the Paint horses she breeds and raises. Turkeys and chickens are her latest interest. She has been teaching her granddaughter to ride horses and pick up chicken eggs. Judy's Leather Shop is thriving so much that she doesn't advertise anymore. While it's still a little weak, Judy's thumb has improved greatly. "There's no use in fretting over things," she says, "you just have to adapt."

BABE (FAITH JEWEL PEARL) MONTGOMERY passed away September 10, 2004. Babe had many lives. At one time she ran a packhorse business in Winthrop and was a caretaker at Sun Mountain Lodge, where she lived with her mother. She also managed a hotel in Tacoma, Washington, for many years. Babe had a talent with horses, teaching her father's plow horse to do tricks when she was a young girl. She was a jockey and a trainer of racehorses. In World War II she drove trucks for the army. Later, she worked at Boeing. She enjoyed reading, storytelling, and stirring things up.

During the summer and fall, MARVA MOUNTJOY cooks for a variety of packers. Packing into the wilderness is still one of her favorite things to do. She recently moved to the Twin Lakes area of Winthrop when her husband, Jim, retired. She keeps busy with her two grandchildren and volunteer work at the local high school.

LAURALEE NORTHCOTT teaches third grade at the local elementary school. Her band, Horse Crazy, just completed their third compact disc. She hosts "The Dollar Watch Cowboy Show" on the radio each Sunday evening. Lauralee works as a freelance cook, often hired by outfitters not only for her culinary expertise but for her storytelling ability.

While it was hard to leave Rocking Horse Ranch, MEGHAN SULLIVAN now manages Bear Creek Equestrian Center in Winthrop, Washington, a thirty-one-acre horse boarding/training facility. She boards and trains horses. Meghan also provides lessons to children and adults. Eventually, she hopes to host clinics for outside instructors. In 2004 Dave Swenson, her husband, started the Rocking Horse Bakery in Winthrop. Meghan sings with the Earthtones.

Index

scapegoat, 112, 118; violence in, 130, 136; women in cowboy culture of, 108, 124. *See also* American West; greenhorns; humor; stories; tourism

Three-Finger Jack's restaurant, 20, 93, 94

Tolton, Debbie, 4

Tompkins, Jane, 15–16, 55

tourism: aggressive humor towards tourists, 57–59, 115–16, 119, 121; American West and, xiii, 14–15, 18–20, 140, 142; assuming tourist mask, 36, 43–44, 45; authenticity, 19, 30–45, 112; cowboy culture and, 2, 15, 17, 22–28, 116–23, 153n9; economic factors of, 14, 18, 42, 45, 59, 103, 116, 147; fantasy and, 27–28, 40, 98–99, 117, 121, 141–42, 153n9; horsewomen, humor, and, 23, 44–45, 88, 91–92, 98–99, 105, 117–23, 150n5; performance for, 29–30, 44, 121–22, 140; pseudoevents, 20, 29–32; sexual harassment and, 96, 98, 101–3, 106; social position and, 42, 59, 64–65, 133–34, 140–44, 150–51n7; tourist ignorance, 35, 37–40, 81, 83, 95, 100, 107, 120–21; Winthrop Westernization and, 13, 17–22, 45, 112, 151–52n7. *See also* American West; Code of the West; cowboys; cowgirls; horsewomen; humor; jokes; stories; tall tales

"Tourist Studies in Anthropological Perspective" (Nuñez), 42

transcription of stories, xv–xvi, 12, 87–88

U.S. Forest Service, 74, 152n9

Virginian, The (Wister), 16

Wagner, Kathryn, 18, 22

Wagner, Otto, 18

Walker, Nancy: humor, 59, 89, 106, 107, 108, 116, 133; tall tales, 130, 131; women's humor, 124, 142

Wanted Dead or Alive: The American West in Popular Culture (Bindas), 26

Welter, Barbara, 131–32

West, John O., 59, 107–8, 133–34

Western accent, xvi, 22–23, 150n1, 153n8

Western clothing, 29, 60, 64, 87, 111, 150n5, 151n4; dressing up, 30–31

Western Horsemen, 5

Weston, Jack, 52–53

wilderness: authority in, 102; cowboy culture and, 16, 127; dangers of, 45, 86; horsewomen's work in, 105, 129, 141; inappropriate behavior in, 101–5; women in, 51, 54

Wister, Owen, 16

"Women and the Language of Men" (Tompkins), 55

work of horsewomen. *See* horsewomen; tourism; wilderness

wranglers, xiv–xv, 2

Yaken, Mary, 109, 111